GET OFF YOUR CUSHION

WEAVING MEDITATION INTO THE FABRIC OF LIFE

LI-ANNE TANG, PH.D.

To all my teachers,
who taught me the joys of patience and perseverance
through their wisdom and compassion.

Ehipassiko
(Come and see for yourself)

THE BUDDHA

CONTENTS

Foreword   viii
Sayadaw U Tejaniya and MaThet Ghosh

Acknowledgments   x

Prologue: My Story   xiii

PART ONE
**THE 5 MISSING INGREDIENTS TO
LIVING FREE FROM STRESS**

1. Stress and Seeking   3
2. Awareness and Alignment   5
3. Urgency and Unflappability   7
4. Compass and Course Correction   9
5. Enjoyability and Environment   11

PART TWO
STRESS A LITTLE LESS

1. Suffering from Stress Is Optional   15
2. Mind the Gaps of Your Mind   23
3. Urgency Without Being in a Hurry   32
4. A Compass for Your Life   39
5. What Fires Together Wires Together   47

PART THREE
FREEDOM FROM SUFFERING

1. The Unconscious Ascetic   57
2. Walking the Path   65
3. The Devil Is in the Details   75
4. The Singular Cause of Your Suffering   85
5. Freeing the Mind   93

Epilogue: Your Turn   103
Glossary   105
About the Author   109
Bonus Material   111

FOREWORD
SAYADAW U TEJANIYA AND
MATHET GHOSH

There are two things I consider absolutely essential for a successful Dhamma practice: the right attitude and daily practice.

When I teach I often observe that the problem is not that yogis are not mindful enough but that they don't have enough of the right attitude. Yogis are also confused about where they are in their practice and wonder what steps they should take next.

Li-Anne has written a book that addresses both these issues in a systematic way. First she shows how to build the right attitude as a daily practice. This is essential because it will help the mind appreciate the journey of awareness. Then Li-Anne provides practical advice on how to handle the most common doubts and pitfalls. Lastly, she explores practical applications of awareness and wise attention in daily life.

So learn to develop the right attitude from Li-Anne and enjoy practising every day!

SAYADAW U TEJANIYA

Have you ever returned home from a meditation retreat and quickly wondered why it was so difficult to keep up the practice in real life?

If you are one of these people, this book is definitely for you. This is the Dhamma book that I have been waiting for, a book that tells you how to apply meditation in everyday life without getting out of touch with life. This book translates the exercises of formal meditation into practical, easy to follow steps. It answers questions and addresses doubts which come up in your practice.

The most significant difference this book has made for my own practice is that it has given me tools to apply the right attitude. Right attitude is an essential, even indispensable part of Dhamma practice, a habit of the mind that we can nurture and cultivate.

In the past I often felt that I not only lacked a positive mindset but that I also did not have a path to learn to develop it. Implementing the very simple steps suggested in this book has helped me immensely to gain a positive mental attitude.

Best of all, this book merits reading over and over again. Each read will reveal more finely how you can incorporate the steps of Dhamma practice into your life in increasingly skilful ways.

May the right attitude help you discover the joys of Dhamma practice!

MATHET GHOSH, INTERPRETER FOR
SAYADAW U TEJANIYA FOR 25+
YEARS

ACKNOWLEDGMENTS

Refuge:

> *Buddham saranam gacchāmi*
> *Dhammam saranam gacchāmi*
> *Sangham saranam gacchāmi*

I would never have been able to write and publish this book without the care and support of many people.

First, I'd like to thank my wonderful husband, Dimitri, for encouraging me to publish this book. I am grateful for the past 36 years we have spent together. I look forward to the next 36 years …

Ma Thet Ghosh, my dear *Dhamma* friend, who has supported me not just in the multiple edits of this book but also my very worst illnesses over the years, words cannot express my gratitude to you. I thank you from the bottom of my heart.

I am eternally grateful to my *Dhamma* teachers over the decades of my practice. In particular, I would like to acknowledge the huge role the following teachers have played in my understanding of the *Dhamma*: Sayadaw U Tejaniya, Culadasa, Sayadaw U Thuzana, Patrick Kearney, Guy Armstrong, Ariya Baumann, Venerable Dhammajiva, Bhante Sujiva, Ajahn Brahm, Shaila Catherine and Thich Nhat Hanh. I hope this book is worthy of the wisdom and compassion you have shared with me.

I would like to thank my numerous editors, who have all

encouraged me through this process in their various different ways: Walter Köchli, Ma Thet Ghosh, Carol Wilson, Sky Dawson, Andrew Sherbrooke, Darlene Tataryn, Eric Lindo and Thomas Hauck. In particular, I would like to express my immense gratitude to Walter, who painstakingly went through this manuscript multiple times with as much care and compassion as he has skill and scholarship.

I wrote the first draft of my prologue and published it online, asking people if they had any questions they would like me to address in the book. Thank you, readers, for the hundreds of questions. I have attempted to answer every one of them.

Finally, I would like to thank my children, my students and my friends, who continue to show me how much more I can learn about this very precious and beautiful life.

PROLOGUE: MY STORY

I was eight years old. In my mind, I knew and felt only suffering. My life was *The Scream* of Edvard Munch. Obstinately determined, I made a pact with myself to find a way out of the unbearable pain of being. One day, I ran away from home and stumbled across a Buddhist temple. That was the day I discovered the teachings that clearly illuminated this way.

Fast forward 28 years. I had become a dedicated meditator and was spending most of my life cultivating my mind. I was no longer the scared and confused child, the angry and tormented teenager, or the seeker and scholar of my twenties. I had finally found my path in life and was living it unreservedly.

After over a decade of searching, I had found a wise teacher who was willing and able to guide me to awakening, to freedom from suffering. This teacher was the Burmese monk Sayadaw U Thuzana, a traditional Buddhist monk who taught in the Mahasi tradition. He moved and spoke mindfully and slowly, and every time I looked him in the eyes during our interviews, it felt like I was looking into infinity. There is no other way I can describe the feeling of looking into the portal to the universe through someone's eyes. My teacher's job was literally to be my sherpa in my pursuit of the pinnacle of the Buddhist path—enlightenment. How cool a job was that!

I was not going to let this opportunity slip me by. I dedicated myself to the task. I meditated two hours each day and attended 2 x 2-week meditation retreats every year. In between, I continued my exploration of Western psychology. In my twenties, I had completed a bachelor of psychology, a master's degree in cognitive science, and a Ph.D. in neuropsychiatry, and was now also exploring the depths of psychoanalytic psychotherapy while raising my two young children.

I knew I was living my calling. Yet, because it was an unconventional one, I had to constantly clear the path to make it my own. It was already unusual to be so unconditionally called to a spiritual life from a young age. But I was also unwaveringly called to be the best mother for my children as was humanly possible, in a way that only someone with the determination of a dog digging up a lost bone could muster.

I frequently felt pulled in the different directions of my spiritual life and my maternal responsibilities. I wholeheartedly wanted to spend my life meditating in my teacher's monastery exactly as much as I wanted to dedicate myself to my children.

But then I encountered what is frequently known as the Dark Night period of my practice. In the midst of a meditation sit I was suddenly facing what I can only describe as utter terror. The traumas of my past were suddenly catching up with me and there was no way around this. It was officially diagnosed as PTSD in the Western psychological world, and the Dark Night of the Soul in the spiritual arena. Here is an excerpt from a diary entry of the time, which I called Memoirs of a Petrified Rabbit:

> *It is nighttime, and there is a fair bit of traffic on the country road. In the middle of the road, a little white rabbit cowers beneath axle after axle of car after car rolling above it. No one has rolled onto it—yet. Surely it is safe now? The rumble of another car approaches. Another near miss. Will this ever end? If so, what then? What becomes of life that follows such an ordeal?*
>
> *I saw this rabbit a few weeks ago. Mine was one of the cars that engulfed it momentarily, and possibly forever more. If I could have, I would have stopped all the traffic behind me with my body, picked up the poor little white rabbit, and laid its quivering body against my chest for as long as it took to help it feel safe again. I would have spent days upon days cradling it with my undivided love and attention, reminding it of a time in the seemingly distant past when all was well.*
>
> *But I couldn't. I had to drive on, for there was a continuous flow of traffic behind me. I remain as one with this rabbit because my life is what follows an ordeal that, although physically different, was experienced in a very similar way.*
>
> *I am the petrified rabbit.*

Necessity is the mother of invention. I needed to learn to deal with this and learn fast. I felt like I could die at any moment, and I was not going to leave this earth defeated—I was way too stubborn to let that happen! Psychotherapy helped the interpersonal and practical challenges I was facing, but my meditation teacher's guidance was what ultimately led to the first of several insights into the reality of our existence.

I followed my teacher's instructions to a T. I didn't feel I had any choice in the matter. It was as if I had been safely in the comfort of an aeroplane in one moment, and in the next I was in free fall. As I plunged down, down, down towards the earth, the only thing I knew for certain was that I was not going to be on that plane again. My life was never going to be the same.

Like Alice in Wonderland, I had stumbled down the rabbit hole. There was nothing else to do. I needed to learn to be with this feeling of utter terror. I needed to learn to make friends with it, to understand it, and ultimately transcend it.

With the gentle and patient guidance of my wise teacher, I did. I learnt to explore the very universal reality of fear through the eyes of a viewer watching a David Attenborough documentary about a petrified rabbit's experience of utter terror, while simultaneously experiencing the terror. Through my meditation practice, I became intrigued and curious about my experiences, and slowly learnt not to be terrified as I continued to fall into the abyss of the unknown. And finally, l learnt not to succumb to the fear of fear itself.

I was lucky that my mind was ripe enough to be able to work through the stages of insights along the traditional Mahasi system and, with the guidance of numerous very experienced teachers, progressed along the path in a typical manner. I remember being on Day 4 of a retreat and reporting to my teacher the fact that the contents of my entire life were spontaneously being reviewed in my mind, which had begun since the arising of an insight the day before. I described the feeling that my life up to that point had comprised crooked bars, but these had now inextricably been straightened. I now saw the world from a vantage I had hitherto never before encountered, and many small details of my life were flashing through my mind in rapid succession from a perspective of clear understanding and compassion. My teacher smiled knowingly and said calmly to me, 'Yes, these reviews only ever happen a few times. Enjoy it while it lasts and see how your life pans out in the next 6-12 months'.

There it was, stated as factually and simply as things can ever be stated. Deeply understanding the *Dhamma* as taught by the Buddha is attainable. There are very distinct, seismic shifts that can happen for people truly committed to this path long term. Such enduring changes in one's worldview are the only proof in the *Dhamma* pudding.

There was no turning back now. This was my new normal. Any semblance of the word 'suffering' seemed irrelevant to my life now. I had been extricated from the burden of my self-created suffering, but before too long I began to suspect that this was simply the start of my real journey. I now knew there was yet more work to be done. There was still a sense of unsatisfactoriness in my existence that I caught a whiff of, albeit intermittently. This was not the end of the path.

I increasingly became more and more aware of some inconsistencies in my life. I approached one thing at a time but felt there was a lack of integration of the various facets of my life. I didn't exactly feel strongly pulled in different directions as I had before, but there was definitely a lack of full alignment in my life.

I had started teaching meditation with the encouragement of my teacher. I continued to raise my children in the best way possible, worked as a psychotherapist and counsellor for patients diagnosed with cancer, and deepened my explorations into psychoanalytic psychotherapy. And I continued to practise towards full liberation. But these felt like disconnected paths in my life.

Unfortunately, my traditional mentors were no longer able to provide guidance on this. My monastic teachers only knew the path to awakening through renunciation of worldly pursuits. I was obviously not going to abandon my children to ordain and complete my spiritual journey. None of the lay teachers I knew had children and were not able to advise on the seemingly mundane but extraordinarily important matters of raising children while on this path. And don't get me started on what I thought when I was told that women were not able to become fully enlightened!

I met Sayadaw U Tejaniya in 2008. His teachings were unconventional and a real game changer for me. His approach was to make mindfulness a way of life. Rather than thinking of meditation as an activity you do sitting on a cushion with your eyes closed, he taught me how to cultivate continuity of mindfulness throughout my daily life. This was the missing link to my practice!

As it turned out, prior to the retreat, I was somewhat torn about whether I should attend it. I had heard of this monk and was very keen to learn all I could from him, but the retreat corresponded with my son's audition for a music scholarship, and I really wanted to support him for this. After discussing it with my eleven-year-old son, with a somewhat guilty heart, I chose to attend the retreat.

At the retreat, from the very first day, we were encouraged to leave the meditation schedule behind, walk at a normal pace during walking meditations and explore off the cushion practices more. We were encouraged to explore our senses, notice our mind states, and build our awareness more continuously throughout our waking hours. We were even encouraged to meditate while talking!

Towards the end of the week, I was amazed at how natural this all felt. My teacher told stories of householders in Burma going to the temple to learn his methods before going back to their busy lives to really implement them. He said that our everyday lives were the best places to practise and encouraged us to apply the methods at home and then report to him. I was intrigued and immediately wanted to try, with his guidance. I asked if I would be allowed to go home to explore these teachings each day for the rest of the retreat time and come back to the meditation centre to report to him each evening. He wholeheartedly encouraged me to do so.

I left the retreat centre with trepidation. This was a total no-no in all the previous retreats I had attended! I got home and was greeted by elated children and a perplexed husband. I explained I was bringing my practice home and going back each evening. And that was exactly how I spent the last few days of the retreat: practising this new way of being in the retreat centre, integrating it into my life, checking in with my teacher, correcting my course as recommended, and then consolidating the practice further in real life.

I learnt to practise in every waking moment of my life. I brought my life to my meditations and my meditations to my life. I finally felt like every effort I made in my life was in service of the same things. My life finally felt aligned and fully on track.

Through this new way of practising, I began to understand this path at a deeper and more nuanced level. And through this practice, I have helped many people eliminate stress, anxiety, and suffering in their lives as well. Some of these people were my meditation students. Others were patients diagnosed with cancer who I was counselling and to whom I did not even mention the words Buddhism, mindfulness, or meditation. I simply helped guide all these people in an efficient, effective, and enjoyable way, just as the Buddha taught.

This powerful practice of continuous mindfulness is surprisingly easy to learn. The effects on reducing stress and anxiety are almost immediate and, as experienced by the numerous students and clients I have helped, result in true progress in the *Dhamma*. The end of suffering is possible, even for lay practitioners—and yes, 'even' for women!

Anyone interested in reducing, and thereafter eliminating stress and suffering from their lives is therefore invited to explore this practice and see for themselves.

PART ONE
THE 5 MISSING INGREDIENTS TO LIVING FREE FROM STRESS

Most of us suffer from stress and believe this is an inevitable part of life. **It is not.** I know this for certain because I have helped hundreds of people to substantially reduce their stress, and dozens to live completely free of it.

Some of these people were very experienced Buddhist meditators aiming for spiritual awakening. Others were patients with cancer, to whom I did not once mention the words 'meditation' or 'mindfulness' but nonetheless taught them the same methods covered in this book. Irrespective of what words are used, all the people seeking my guidance simply wanted to end their stress and suffering.

This practice is both linear and multifaceted. To make it easier to apply, I have divided the book into three parts. This first part, The 5 Missing Ingredients to Living Free from Stress, is very short and emphasises the framework upon which the entire book is structured. Part Two, 'Stress a Little Less,' takes you through the journey from the eyes of a meditator who has been practising for many years, but still suffers a lot from stress and anxiety. This is a typical journey of many of my students, and an essential foundation for beginners and experienced meditators alike.

Part Three of the book, 'Freedom From Suffering,' is more multifaceted in nature. It discusses seemingly different practices through the lens of a practical application of the Four Noble Truths. The entire book emphasises mindfulness off the cushion, in your daily life.

Reflecting on thousands of hours working with many people from all walks of life, I see a theme of five pairs of missing ingredients that prevent people from really living free from stress and suffering. The resulting acronym is the secret SAUCE of navigating the challenges of life.

You will note that strictly speaking, the acronym should be SSAAUUCCCEE. But in life, it's often wiser to choose not what is technically correct but what is simple and pleasing!

CHAPTER 1
STRESS AND SEEKING

L et me start with a definition of what I mean by stress. I refer to any form of discontent, dissatisfaction, or resistance to what you are experiencing in life as stress. In the ancient language of *Pāli*, this is known as *dukkha*.

Perhaps surprisingly, the first missing ingredient to learning to truly live free from stress is the presence of stress itself.

As it turns out, there is a bit of a Goldilocks zone in relation to this. If you are *too* stressed, this can lead to overwhelm and burnout. If you are not sufficiently aware of any discontent, how can you transcend *dukkha*?

If you are too stressed, you need to learn to reduce your stress at will throughout your day. Part Two of this book, 'Stress a Little Less,' teaches you how to automatically reduce your stress, all of the time.

On the other hand, if you are not sufficiently aware of your discontent, you will not be able to truly understand the Buddhist tenet of the First Noble Truth of *dukkha*. The chapter on 'The Unconscious Ascetic' in Part Three of the book explores this in a practical way.

There is a joke that goes:
Q: How many psychotherapists does it take to change a light bulb?
A: One, but the light bulb needs to really want to change.

In my work as a psychotherapist and mindfulness mentor, I know this all too well. *It doesn't matter that there are ways to alleviate stress and suffering; unless someone actively seeks this relief, no teacher or method can be of service to them.* You need to truly seek in order to find the gateway to awakening to a life entirely free from stress.

CHAPTER 2
AWARENESS AND ALIGNMENT

Awareness is central to all of life—and yet it's the biggest deficit we have. We are, of course, ironically not aware of this fact. The reason for cultivating continuity of mindfulness is to build this faculty of awareness to better serve ourselves and the people around us.

To be more *aware* is to be more *conscious*. If we could be more conscious of our thoughts, speech, and actions, this would substantially reduce the suffering we bring to ourselves and others. Increasing awareness will be the central theme of this book as I teach you the subtle art of continuous mindfulness.

One of the things of which we are often unaware is our conflicting desires. On the one hand, you may want to reduce your stress. On the other hand, you may be striving towards a particular goal. These sometimes seem incongruent.

Instead of trying to power ahead while anchored, it may be worth pausing to explore if there is a way to align seemingly conflicting desires. Once you have done this, you can then apply continuous mindfulness to pursue your aligned goals through effortless effort. I discuss practical ways of doing this in the chapters 'Mind the Gaps of Your Mind' of Part Two and 'Walking the Path' of Part Three.

CHAPTER 3
URGENCY AND UNFLAPPABILITY

I spent over a decade helping patients with cancer who, irrespective of prognosis, had the poignant reality of our mortality shoved in front of their faces. The urgency of their plight, for relief from suffering, was palpable. These patients remain some of the most amazing people I have met, in terms of their willingness to change under sometimes extraordinarily difficult circumstances. They have also been the quickest to learn, and I have come to realise that this sense of urgency is a great motivator for true progress.

My meditation students with the same thirst, or spiritual urgency, also reap the fruits of their practice. The students without this sense of urgency seem to plateau or meander in their practice for a very long time. My emphasis on mindfulness off the cushion is an attempt to remind everyone that our precious lives are finite, and it is only in this very moment that we can find liberation from stress and suffering. We don't know how much time we have left on this earth. It could be measured in days, months, or years.

How conscious can you be in this very moment?

Despite this urgency, the practice requires unflappability, the skill of equanimity. Cultivating equanimity is very much part of meditation practice. I discuss the interplay between urgency and unflappability in the chapter 'Urgency Without Being in a Hurry' in Part Two of the book. In Part Three, urgency comes in the form of constant investigation as this is carefully balanced with equanimity.

CHAPTER 4
COMPASS AND COURSE CORRECTION

Many meditators are confused about whether they are making progress, or perhaps frustrated in the knowledge that they are not. The reason is they have drifted off course due to a lack of a good compass and a clear method for course correction.

For a compass to be effective, you need to first know the direction you wish to head. If you need to resist the beckoning of burnout, this is where your compass needs to point. Forget any other lofty ideas you have about meditation or enlightenment; your job is to monitor your 'burnout compass' at all times. If stress and anxiety are what you would like freedom from, have your 'stress and anxiety compass' with you at all times. Alternatively, if a descent into depression is what you most wish to avoid, your 'depression compass' needs to be at your ready.

It may be a 'wisdom compass' or a 'compassion compass' that is most pertinent to you. The idea is to choose the compass that resonates most with your current circumstances, in service of easing your suffering and moving out of the everlasting cycles of stress and relief.

Once you have chosen your compass, regularly check to ensure you are always facing the right direction. For example, if you regularly experience stress and anxiety, be on the lookout for any increased stress during the day and have an aspiration to face the direction of more calm and ease. This is how you cultivate continuous mindfulness.

If you are not facing the direction of calm and relaxation, you will need to course correct. This typically involves a simple 3-step process to head in the right direction again. Even if you are not walking in the direction of your aspiration yet, you are now at least facing this direction. Every step you take from here on will move you towards your goal.

The importance of having a compass and course correction are described in the foundational practice of Chapter 4 of Part Two, 'A Compass for Your Life'. These foundations are refined later in Chapter 4 of Part Three, 'The Singular Cause of Your Suffering'.

CHAPTER 5
ENJOYABILITY AND ENVIRONMENT

A surprising thing most people miss in the pursuit of freedom from suffering is the importance of *enjoyment*. The best way to succeed in anything in life is to enjoy it. If you would like to stress less and incline your mind towards peace and calm, enjoy the moments of relative calm when they are present. It really is as simple as this!

When you enjoy these moments, dopamine, endorphins and serotonin are released and a positive feedback loop is formed in your brain. So, instead of perpetuating pathways of increasing stress, the pathways of relaxation and calm are reinforced. The more often you do this in your daily mindfulness, the stronger these pathways become.

The final chapter of Part Two, 'What Fires Together Wires Together,' talks about how the 3-step process capitalises on this positive reinforcement system of the brain, to form and strengthen new habitual patterns of mind that incline towards calm and relaxation. In the final chapter of the book, I show how realising the Third Noble Truth, completely 'Freeing Our Mind' from stress and suffering, is possible through supportive environments and enjoyment.

> *You can choose how you live. When you cultivate your awareness, you have more options to choose with wisdom. Will you too choose freedom from stress and suffering?*

PART TWO
STRESS A LITTLE LESS

A man we'll call 'Peter' has suffered from anxiety for as long as he can remember. He chanced upon a meditation book in his local library soon after experiencing his first panic attack as a teenager, and has been conscientiously trying to perfect the art ever since.

Soon after college, Peter moved to Silicon Valley to work as a software engineer. Over the years, his work has become more demanding. He is increasingly finding that the effects of his meditations are insufficient to prevent his frequent bouts of feeling overwhelmed, and fears he is on the knife's edge of burnout.

Peter finds it difficult to relax. He gets frustrated at his inability to manage his stress, and fears it's having a deleterious impact on his relationship with his partner and his health. He tends to be very critical of himself and doubles down to 'get things right,' which often exacerbates the situation.

Peter would *like* to believe that suffering from stress is

optional, but in his heart he doesn't. The thought of not being a slave to angst in life is too much in the realm of fantasy for him. All he wants is to suffer a little less.

Part Two of this book follows Peter on his journey, a typical one that many of my students follow.

Whether you would like to suffer a little less or fully realise the end of suffering through awakening, Part Two provides the foundations required for progress on this path. You first need to be able to habitually reduce your stress at will. Only then will you be confident that you can implement the profound and practical system that has been laid out for us. Nothing in this book is original; it's simply my attempt to apply ancient Buddhist wisdom to modern times, based directly on my personal experience and the experiences of hundreds of students with whom I have had the privilege to work.

CHAPTER 1
SUFFERING FROM
STRESS IS OPTIONAL

All Peter wanted to do was *learn to relax*. He simply didn't know how to. When he signed up for a 12-week program and saw the title of the first week, 'Relax and Be Aware,' he was triggered into a panic. The reason he had signed up for this course was because he was far too aware of his stress and anxiety, but unable to relax!

The title of this impossible-to-implement statement seemed to taunt him.

'Relax and be aware? How?' he beseeched himself desperately. The title didn't budge. He clicked on the first video.

He watched through the 15-minute introductory video. It all made sense and seemed easy enough. There was a simple 3-step process that he needed to follow several times each day over the following week:

(1) Notice the level of his stress and assign it a number,

(2) Take it down a notch, and

(3) Smile and congratulate himself.

The rationale was that the first step made him aware of his stress levels, the second reminded him to consciously reduce it, and the third step created a positive reinforcement loop in his brain to make it more likely that he would remember to be aware again in the future, to increase the likelihood of this cycle repeating at a later stage. He tried it, as was instructed.

What is the level of my stress right now?
It's at 7.
Can I take it down a notch?
Yes. Just listening to the calm voice on the video is relaxing. Stress level 4 now.
Smile and congratulate myself?
Ok, I can smile. Hey, it feels good to have succeeded in this. I'll take the congratulation the voice is giving me.

The truth was, being *aware* was not the issue for him. Peter was always acutely aware that he was anxious. In fact, being aware of his anxiety was what often led to the feeling of being overwhelmed. He decided to pose this question to the instructor on the forum. He wrote, 'I am acutely aware that I am anxious, but not able to relax. Help?' He wondered if he would get a satisfactory response.

The response was as follows:

It is very common that people initially feel they are acutely aware of their anxiety and stress, but don't know what to do about this. They freeze like deer in the headlights. Actually, it is worse than that. They become more like kangaroos in the headlights. If you have not driven in outback Australia, you may not know that kangaroos don't just freeze in response to the sight of headlights of oncoming cars, but as the car approaches, they tend to become so confused that they actually hop right in front of the car. What I am trying to show you is a simple process of not getting confused when you are aware of your stress and anxiety, such that you don't inadvertently exacerbate the situation.

Continuing to stare into the headlights of stress and anxiety will increase your confusion about what to do next. This is where giving it a number helps. What is the level of your stress and anxiety now? Recognising the level of stress is the first of the 3-step process. Time for the next step now: take this down a notch.

The issue most people untrained in this process face is they continue to stare at the headlights. Don't. It is time to take this number down a notch by looking in a different direction. Consciously relax your body a bit, take a deep breath in, and try to make the out-breath longer than the in-breath. Do this a couple of times. What is the level of your stress and anxiety now?

If it has dropped to anything less than what it originally was, congratulations! You have succeeded in taking it down a notch. Smile and congratulate yourself for another success! Now rinse and repeat.

Peter tried this throughout the week. Intermittently throughout the day, he identified the level of his anxiety, took a few deeper breaths in and out—making sure he extended the length of the out-breath—and then checked again to see if his anxiety had reduced. The process worked at the start of the week, but later that week, it seemed to be no longer working and he started feeling increasingly more agitated.

He decided to watch the next set of videos, to see if they would shed light on this process. Some other students in the pre-recorded videos seemed to encounter similar issues. The response was always a calm and confident repeat of the same three instructions, sometimes emphasising one of the three steps more than the others to highlight the aspect the student had somehow skipped over.

> *Q: Is it difficult to know the level of stress or anxiety you*
> *are experiencing?*
> *A: No.*
> *Q: Good. That is Step 1. Now, Step 2: can you take it*
> *down a notch by taking a couple of deeper breaths?*
> *A: Yes, but I'm still anxious.*
> *Q: Has the number gone down at all?*
> *A: Yes, but it's still high. I'm still anxious.*

This was the gist of Peter's experience as well. The response was the first game-changer in this process for him.

> *It doesn't matter if the level of your stress and anxiety moved*
> *from 8 to 0, or from 8 to 7 ¾. The fact that it has moved in the*
> *right direction is what you are aiming to do. Your only aim is to*
> *incline your mind towards relaxation. You have succeeded*
> *whenever you are no longer facing the direction of more stress*
> *and anxiety, but instead inclining towards more ease and relax-*
> *ation. Once you are facing the right direction, every step you*
> *take will be towards your goal of more peace in your life.*

Somehow, this made sense to Peter. The aim is to face the right direction. The instruction was simply to take the level of anxiety down a notch. And the suggested method was to direct his attention to a couple of longer breaths.

This set of surprisingly simple instructions seemed to work very well. But before long, Peter's brain was no longer able to handle this level of simplicity. Surely there is more to life than this? 'Taking things down a notch' was fine initially, but he needed more to chew on!

As the week progressed, he increasingly became more agitated at the process.

'I can take it down a notch,' he thought, 'but now what? It's not as if I have managed to rid myself of the stresses of life!'

The next set of instructions seemed to read his mind. There was a discussion that emphasised a big distinction between *attention* and *awareness*. These two common words are often used interchangeably in meditation instructions. Peter was confused. He had often heard the meditation instruction 'put your attention or focus on your breath'. The video seemed to imply that this instruction was different from 'be aware of your breath.' Why was there so much emphasis on differentiating attention from awareness?

These were the instructions:

Whenever you focus your attention on something, it dominates your conscious experience. At the same time, though, you can be more generally aware of things in the background. For example, right now your attention is focused on listening to what I am saying. At the same time, though, you're also aware of what I look like and perhaps how you may be feeling. You can be aware of, or know, lots of different things simultaneously, but your attention can only rest on one thing at a time.

You can pay attention and have awareness simultaneously because these two faculties are associated with two different brain networks that process information in fundamentally different ways. Paying attention involves a bilateral dorsal network of structures in the brain. Narrow and sharply focused attention allows us to see discrete details. These structures of the brain are also involved in verbal, intentional, conceptual, and evaluative processes.

Awareness, on the other hand, involves a right-lateralised ventral network of brain structures. These structures provide an open, panoramic awareness that automatically orientates to new stimuli, and can disengage and re-direct attention. These areas of the brain are only minimally verbal; rather, they are mainly sensorial and non-judgmental in nature. These are the 'it just is' parts of the brain. The main thing these two systems have in common is that both contribute to our conscious experience.

Let's play with attention and awareness a bit now to see if you can differentiate the two processes. Look away from the screen now and choose to put your attention on something nearby. In other words, find something to look at, and look at it. See the shape, colour, and finer details of whatever you are looking at. Can you also notice that you don't just see whatever you have chosen to look at, but you can also see the things around it? You can also hear what I am saying, despite the fact you are consciously looking at the object. So, even though your attention is on what you are looking at, you can simultaneously be aware of other things.

Have a look at the screen again now. You may ask, why is this bit of information important? It is important because knowing this will allow you to get the benefits of meditation, on and off the cushion, more efficiently, effectively, and effortlessly.

Let me give you an example. When you start meditating, you are frequently asked to direct your attention on your breath. You now know that attention is only one part of the equation in meditation. Awareness is just as, if not more, important. So, while your attention is on your breath, be aware of how tense or relaxed your body feels. If it feels relaxed, enjoy it.

If it feels tense, relax your body a bit ... and smile to yourself for a job well done.

Try this for yourself now. Can you notice the level of tension or relaxation in your body as you are watching this video? Do what you need to do to consciously relax your body down a notch. You don't have to be totally relaxed; just a little more relaxed than a moment ago. Now smile to yourself because you have succeeded in inclining your mind towards relaxation.

This simple, 3-step process works all the time. You become aware of the tension and do whatever you need to do to take it down a notch. And then you smile to yourself for a job well done. It's not really that difficult, is it? Now enjoy the feeling of greater relaxation.

I'll go through this again. Use awareness to notice the level of tension in your body and bring in your attention to consciously relax the body a little bit. Now smile and give yourself a pat on the back. Don't forget this part, because this seemingly simple step serves as a very powerful positive reinforcement for your brain, and positive reinforcement is the most effective way for your brain to learn new habits. So if you want to connect with peace and wisdom all of the time, start by learning to incline your mind towards greater relaxation.

Peter was born with a good head for numbers, but the rest of life generally made him very anxious. He remembered memorising the digits of *pi* to 56 decimal places as a child, and every time he was anxious at school, he recited them in his head.

The distinction between attention and awareness somehow made sense to him. When he was anxious at school, he had instinctively placed his attention on reciting the digits of *pi,* which shifted his attention from the anxiety he felt to the process of reciting. He clearly remembers how this calmed his nervous system down. So the process of reducing stress at will has something to do with consciously placing your attention onto something—anything—that moves in a direction away from stress and toward calm. It doesn't matter if it's reciting the digits of *pi* or your breath, as long as you're not staring at the headlights of anxiety or jumping in front of it, this is the right direction.

Peter felt empowered with this new information. He now knew that he needed to be more conscious, or aware, of where his attention was. Wherever his attention pointed to was the direction he was facing. Is this the direction towards peace and calm, or towards more stress and anxiety? Success is when you turn towards the right direction.

CHAPTER 2
MIND THE GAPS OF
YOUR MIND

"What can we gain by sailing to the moon if we are not able to cross the abyss that separates us from ourselves? This is the most important of all voyages of discovery, and without it, all the rest are not only useless, but disastrous."

THOMAS MERTON

Peter has always been a bit of a perfectionist, and often becomes frustrated at himself whenever he doesn't 'get things right.' If he were to sum up his main difficulty, he would say that it is his anxiety. If I were to sum up Peter's main difficulty, I would suggest that it's his frustration with himself at not always meeting his high expectations, which ends up resulting in increased anxiety.

The next instruction on the videos was to bring mindfulness (a.k.a. awareness) more regularly throughout his day. Peter knew this was going to be his undoing. How on earth was he going to remember to be aware of his stress and anxiety levels throughout the day, when life and work were so hectic?

The videos explained things logically and rationally, and he enjoyed the guided meditations that immediately put the theory into practice. But as the week progressed, Peter became more and more frustrated at his lack of ability to have continuous mindfulness throughout the day.

He was anxious about attending the twice-monthly mentoring group scheduled for that week, but decided to join and just sit in on it with his video off. He had considered simply watching a replay of the online course but was so frustrated at not being able to achieve continuity of mindfulness that he decided he might bring his struggle up in the session.

The session was run like a coaching mastermind where everyone was given a chance to discuss their practice and receive individualised guidance. Peter decided to bite the bullet, turn on his video, and raise his Zoom hand. He was extremely nervous about this, but he really wanted to take this opportunity to learn. He explained his difficulties as succinctly as possible, and received this response.

My very first instruction to you was to Relax and Be Aware. This is the most important step. Consciously relax your body, take a deep breath in, and an even deeper breath out. Do this again. Now notice if you are more relaxed. Are you? Good. Now smile to yourself for a job well done. You have managed to incline your mind towards more calm and relaxation.

There seems to be some internal conflict or misalignment here. On the one hand, you'd like to learn to live with less stress and anxiety. On the other hand, because you have a tendency towards perfectionism, every time you are less than perfect, you tend to become frustrated with yourself. This frustration possibly turns to agitation, stress, and anxiety. Does that ring true to you?

Peter had to admit that this seemed to be the process that he very regularly went through. There was a perpetual anxiety that seemed to underlie his very being, but could this be related to his perfectionism? More importantly, what could he do about it? Was he forever doomed to stress and anxiety?

The instructor continued:

We can call perfectionism a tendency of your mind. I would guess that it has both served you well and been the bane of your existence. It has served you in all the things you have succeeded in doing. You would not be in the job you are in, achieved all you have, without wanting to improve yourself. This desire to improve yourself is the very reason you are at this course. You will succeed in learning to live with less stress and anxiety because of this very tendency.

But you need to be more aware when this tendency rears its head and takes over, forcing you in the opposite direction. This is exactly why we are building your awareness. So, when you recognise that you are facing the direction of more stress and anxiety, redirect your attention to relax your body and consciously take the level of anxiety down a notch. Take a moment to enjoy the temporary reprieve and savour your success in heading in the right direction again.

Now, ask yourself: 'What is happening now? What am I experiencing in this moment?' You may notice sounds around you. You may be conscious of sensations in your body. You may be aware of your general mood, the temperature around you, or the sights around you. You may even be aware that you are hearing, seeing, or sitting. There are a plethora of things you can be aware of.

So, right now, what are you aware of?

Peter responded that he was aware that it was a nice, sunny day with a perfect temperature. He noticed that he was experiencing a lot less anxiety and actually feeling quite comfortable.

Great! You're on track again. You are aware, and this is exactly what we are trying to cultivate. Enjoy connecting to your sentience. If perfectionism is a tendency of yours, please take the phrase 'continuity of mindfulness' with a pinch of salt. Think of this as building a 'momentum of mindfulness' instead.

There will be times during your day that you will completely forget about this practice. This is to be expected. We are looking to build a new habit, and it takes time to do this. The moment you remember to be mindful, ask yourself, 'What is happening right now?'

The question is a prompt for you to connect to your actual experiences of life in this very moment. This kick-starts the process of being aware again. Does this feel doable?

It did. And so Peter spent the week building a momentum of mindfulness. Intermittently during the day, he would either ask himself, 'What is happening right now?' or if he already knew he was stressed, he asked himself, 'What is the level of my anxiety right now?' before taking it down a notch. His week became noticeably more pleasant, and he was proud of himself for actually making a positive difference to his state of well-being.

In one of the following week's videos, another student said that when she asked herself the question, 'What is happening right now?' she felt overwhelmed at noticing a lot of things. She explained that she was autistic and frequently felt overwhelmed by life. She said that her experience of life was that everything felt very 'loud' and intrusive, and she felt building mindfulness was the very opposite of what she needed.

The response was as follows:

I have worked with many neurodiverse people over the decades. I understand how general instructions to a neurotypical population can sometimes seem counter-productive.

The important thing to remember is the direction you would like to head.

You'd like to be less overwhelmed by life. This is your first priority. Any time you are heading in the direction of more anxiety, you know that this is the direction that leads to feeling overwhelmed. Your efforts should be to face the other direction, towards less anxiety. Using the word 'calm' is probably too much of a stretch in these times, so just think of facing the direction of 'less anxiety.'

What is the level of your anxiety? Give it a number. This is the only thing you need to be aware of. Now, direct your attention to consciously relax your body a bit. Bring the anxiety down just a notch. Take a few deeper breaths, keeping your attention on how your body feels as you breathe in and out. What's the level of your stress now? A little lower? Well done. Smile to yourself for succeeding in moving in the right direction.

It is important to implement the right practice for the right circumstance. If you already know that you are stressed and anxious, the only additional thing you need to be aware of is the level of this anxiety. Then your next task is to consciously take it down a notch. And don't forget to enjoy the relief of less anxiety.

If you are constantly anxious, let anxiety be the way you develop continuous mindfulness. Using anxiety as your barometer, regularly monitor your level of anxiety, bring it down a notch and enjoy the reprieve each and every time you succeed.

If you are not constantly anxious, the question 'What is happening right now' kick-starts the process of tuning in to awareness. The reality is, it doesn't matter what you are aware of; as long as you are aware, you are on the right track to suffering a little less.

Peter implemented the suggestions and found the kick-starting process helped create a nice momentum of mindfulness. He was feeling like he was really getting the hang of this when suddenly it all seemed to fall to pieces.

'Why can't I get it anymore?' he thought. 'I am so useless. This always happens to me. I start something, it goes well, and then I find out it doesn't work. Maybe this method isn't the right thing for me. Maybe I need to read that book I came across the other day. Maybe it's time to move to the next shiny object ....' More and more thoughts formed in his head and started spiralling out of control.

He posed a question to the forum: 'Is this working for you?' and explained his situation.

Some people responded with some helpful suggestions. Others commiserated. Then the teacher responded.

You mentioned that you had managed to create a nice momentum of mindfulness just before things fell apart. Could there have been an expectation that this momentum needed to continue? Remember that the aim is to cultivate awareness. The process is simple. You start with the question 'What is happening right now?' and tune in to whatever you can notice at this moment. You are back on track now.

Sometimes, this will build into a momentum of flow. Enjoy this when it happens. But there is constant flux in life, and this momentum will not continue. This is not a problem, because you can simply be aware of the shifting gears of your mindfulness. This awareness itself is the important part; what you are aware of (be it flow or non-flow) is not important. The fact that you are aware is what you want to connect with.

The fact that you could report the process of getting into flow, losing the flow, getting frustrated, being critical and blaming on yourself, doubting yourself and the practice, wanting to look for a different silver bullet, and so on, clearly demonstrates that you were aware to a certain extent. You simply wouldn't be able to describe the process if you were not conscious.

I know it doesn't feel like this for you at the moment, but this is actually really good. I am not saying that it is good that you are frustrated. I am saying that it is good that you are aware of this. Because being aware is better than the alternative of being unconscious of what is happening within you. So celebrate the awareness and tune in to this reality.

This was another game changer for Peter. Being aware of whatever his unwieldy mind was doing was good! He could either be in the unwieldiness of it or be aware of it. He could either be self-critical or aware this was happening. The relief was palpable. He could feel a space between him and his thoughts. He was 'back on track' again, as the teacher put it.

The week progressed very well. Peter felt like he was flowing through life, in touch with everything that was happening but not caught up with anything. He continued watching the videos in the course, which touched on many problems he encountered and others he didn't even realise he faced. He decided to write an entry in his journal to reflect on what he had learnt.

The constant reminders in the videos help me stop believing all my unhelpful and self-critical thoughts. This has been a major epiphany for me. I have always believed that just because I thought something, it was true. I now see that there are two ways to relate to any thought: believing it or simply knowing that it's happening.

Thoughts can be so sticky! Especially the self-critical and negative ones. Learning to recognise that I am thinking, just saying to myself 'Thinking is happening,' gives me some distance from the thoughts. What a relief!

Sure, I'll forget again and then get sucked into a spiral of a negative thinking pattern, but this is part of the practice. The practice is about being aware of this. It is only from this space of awareness that I have a choice to continue believing the thought or place my attention on something else.

When I'm thinking at work and trying to solve a problem, the thoughts are obviously useful. I can recognise that thinking is happening, perhaps take a moment to take my stress levels down a notch and go back to the thinking. If, on the other hand, I'm lying in bed swimming in thoughts about how to solve the same problem, the thoughts are not useful for the purpose of falling asleep. When I realise I'm thinking these useless thoughts, I can choose to direct my attention onto something else, such as any sensations I feel in my body.

I can feel the warmth of the bed, the softness of the sheets, the heaviness of my body. I keep my attention on these aspects of my experience. Every time I realise I am stuck in a thought, I smile to the awareness for highlighting this fact, relax my body, and redirect my attention to the aspects of my sensations that help sleep envelop me. This is no different from meditating on a cushion; the aim is to use awareness to direct my attention onto something that is beneficial, not detrimental. When it's appropriate to try to fall asleep, I should not be thinking. I've always known this, but now I have something concrete I can be doing to create the conditions that are conducive to sleep.

There is one more thing that has changed in me. I think I have always used my meditation practice to try to fix something that I feel is inherently 'wrong' with me. I am slowly coming to the realisation that I am basically okay— 'perfect in all my imperfection,' as my teacher puts it. I find comfort in hearing my teacher's voice in my head regularly reminding me of this.

'Whatever you are experiencing, can this be okay, just for this moment?'

CHAPTER 3
URGENCY WITHOUT BEING IN A HURRY

"To reach a port we must sail, sometimes with the wind, and sometimes against it. But we must not drift or lie at anchor."

OLIVER WENDELL HOLMES, SR.

One month after starting the course, Peter felt like a different man. He was no longer constantly anxious, and could now 'take things down a notch' at will. He was appreciating more and more things in life, was kinder to himself, and noticeably more present and engaged with the people around him. Life flowed beautifully.

Suddenly at work, the you-know-what hit the fan. Peter's team was in a panic. There was a major flaw in the software system they were developing that needed to be fixed. He reflected that just a month earlier, he would have stayed up all night to try to fix the problem. Now he could clearly see that he would be more effective at fixing things after a good night's sleep. He had garnered enough momentum in his practice to continue engaging it in a way that would allow him to sleep. His overthinking had previously often prevented him from sleeping, but now he knew exactly what he needed to do when this happened.

He was reminded of a phrase his teacher had used in one of the sessions: 'urgency without being in a hurry.' Yes, there was definitely urgency in this situation, but he needed to take things one step at a time to ensure he did not feel overwhelmed and botch things up—for himself personally and for the project. He knew it was essential to have a very clear and calm mind.

Peter remembered the teachings about attention and awareness. Awareness brings clarity and perspective, while attention brings serenity and focus. He needed to engage both his eagle eye and his hawk eye to solve this problem. He considered the problem from a big-picture perspective (awareness) and clearly saw what needed to be done. Then he set himself to the task of working on each detail, one at a time (attention).

When the task started feeling overwhelming, which he noticed through his constant mindfulness of his level of stress, Peter smiled in appreciation of his awareness for alerting him to this fact, and gently shifted his attention to taking a couple of deeper, more conscious breaths to 'take things down a notch.' Then he reminded himself to put a maximum of three things on his focus list. Any more would be overwhelming. 'One thing at a time' rang his teacher's voice in his head. He continued, fully focused on one thing, and only afterwards, on the next.

Things got done. Occasionally, he would take a bigger perspective on the situation, acknowledge, and appreciate the progress he had made, and give himself a pat on the back. His teacher had stressed how important this step was. It felt good to be able to see how much progress he had made, and this feeling of satisfaction gave him the energy to do the next task at hand.

Calmly and confidently, Peter effectively fixed the problem in a surprisingly efficient and enjoyable manner. When it was all over, he reflected on the process and how much progress he had made in his practice. What had changed in him? What was he doing differently? How could he ensure he continued along this path? What would he need to do to prevent sliding back into old habits?

Peter reflected on his new ability to be comfortable in the face of uncertainty. Not that long ago, in the face of this situation he would have been flooded with anxiety. Sure, the uncertainty of the enormity of things still felt very uncomfortable, but he had somehow learnt to *be* comfortable in the face of discomfort.

An analogy of a satellite popped into his head. It was as if awareness were a satellite orbiting around the experiences of life. In this case, awareness orbited around the feeling of discomfort in the face of uncertainty.

Whenever there was any discomfort (be it anxiety, uncertainty, or anything else), he used to be too close to the feeling of it, burning into the atmosphere, only to crash and merge with the feeling. Now, he had learnt the art of mindfulness—knowing what was happening, while it was happening, no matter what it was—from a space of openness, allowing, and interest. He had learned how to stay in the orbit of his experiences without crashing and burning, but also without drifting off.

Peter now understood that it is entirely possible to feel contentment and simultaneously get things done. They were not mutually exclusive, as he had previously assumed. He didn't need his anxiety to drive him to achieve all he wanted to do in life. He had learnt to trust the process of awareness and saw for himself how learning to relax actually helped him be more effective and efficient in his work. The trick was to remember to relax a little, enjoy the reprieve, and then get back to the task at hand—one step at a time.

He recalled his teacher's description of mindfulness in a webinar that he had always resonated with, and was now totally attuned to:

> *Imagine a deep, deep ocean. Now, imagine a long rod firmly planted into the very bottom of this ocean. This rod is so long that the other end reaches the surface of the water, protruding into the air. When the external conditions are rough, waves pelt relentlessly against the top of the rod. When the weather is fine, the rod is met with sunshine and gently lapping waves.*
>
> *When you cultivate mindfulness, you are strengthening your connection with this rod. Through strong mindfulness, you learn to weather the storms of life happily and effortlessly, because you always know that although you can't control much of what life dishes out to you, you can control how you experience it. Strong mindfulness is remembering that the rod is always firmly grounded within the deep, still ocean.*
>
> *With proper guidance from an expert in mindfulness, you can develop your skills in mindfulness efficiently and effectively, for all the different circumstances you may encounter in life.*

It really felt true. Peter felt empowered to weather the storms of life through becoming more and more aware. It wasn't just a matter of being mindful when he was sitting in meditation; he had to consistently build a continuity of mindfulness throughout the day to reap the benefits of this practice, such that when the proverbial stuff hit the fan, he could automatically slide into the habit of mindfulness.

He felt he could now tune into the music of life through this practice, and dance with freedom for the first time in his life. How incredibly wonderful and liberating this felt! His relationship with his partner was better than it had ever been. He felt connected with her, and somehow felt this was related to his better connection with, and acceptance of, himself. Various insights into his habitual patterns of mind emerged as he went for walks, relaxed on his outside couch enjoying the brisk breeze cutting through the warm sunshine, and sat in meditation. He was finally on the path he worked so hard for all his life. Who would have thought it would be such a simple and enjoyable way to get back on track?

He reflected on what he might need to do to ensure he continued along this path. He knew the insights he had about the tendencies of his mind were likely to disappear if he did not continue this practice. They were insights of his psychological makeup, the first but very important layer of understanding the habitual patterns of his mind.

He had experienced a few years of psychotherapy in the past, which had helped him come to terms with his complicated relationship with his mother, bullying he had experienced as a child, and finding his place in the world as an adult. His therapist had mentored him, providing him with a role model of how a healthy relationship could be, re-parenting him in a way. This process became instrumental in opening him to the reality of forming a loving and mutually beneficial relationship with his partner. Through therapy, he had learnt to feel more comfortable in his own skin, as well as finding new ways of interacting with people around him. There came a time when he was no longer struggling in his life, and this led to the natural conclusion of the therapy sessions.

Peter always knew there was more to explore. He felt this in the core of his being. He may have come to terms with his life through understanding why he tended to behave in certain ways through exploring his history, but there were still some seemingly intrinsic qualities of his existence that had an air of 'unsatisfactoriness.' He could not pinpoint what exactly this was, nor ascribe a reason to it.

Through this practice of mindfulness, he came to see that analysing this unsatisfactoriness was beyond his capacity to figure out. Asking why his feelings of dissatisfaction existed led to further explorations of the stories of his past that neither brought further relief nor insight.

However, asking how this unsatisfactoriness had arisen brought very interesting results.

Asking 'how' brought Peter to explore the process of his life. While he had previously only been interested in the content of who did what and when, now he was interested in the myriad causes and conditions that seemed to precede any sense of dissatisfaction he felt. He could also start discerning the flavour of dissatisfaction and see the numerous consequences that resulted from its arising.

Whereas he may at times have been bored in his meditation practice of 'just watching the breath,' he was now utterly fascinated by every minute detail of his experiences of life. Even when boredom arose, he became curious and interested in it!

There were, of course, ups and downs. And the tendency to be impatient and expect fast progress reared its head at various times. But Peter had learnt to see through this. Whenever he noticed he was frustrated at a lack of progress, he now smiled to the awareness for doing its job, relaxed his body, and appreciated the fact that he was now orbiting around the experience of frustration, rather than continuing to believe the story of what his mind threw up when he was frustrated, and drowning in it. This qualitative shift occurred frequently and swiftly now.

His practice dropped off a couple of times, and he was surprised at how quickly he fell back into old habits. But as soon as he realised this was happening and turned his attention to the awareness of this fact, he was back in orbit again. No matter how lost he sometimes found himself in his old habits and behaviours, one moment of remembering was all it took to be back on track. This realisation was as liberating as it was empowering.

He wrote an entry in his journal:

> In the face of lots of things that need to be done, I need to maintain the reality of the urgency of the situation while in a state of unflappability. Only then will I be able to get what needs to happen done in an efficient and effective way. I have come to realise that this state of being is also very enjoyable and empowering.
>
> If I am to regularly experience this state, then I must maintain and build continuity of mindfulness throughout my day. The important thing to remember is that I am only ever one step away from coming back. Whenever I find myself stressed, anxious, overwhelmed, or simply unhappy, the very fact that I have noticed that means awareness has done its job. My job is simply to acknowledge the presence of awareness, appreciate it, and enjoy it.

CHAPTER 4
A COMPASS FOR YOUR LIFE

Peter came to realise that his busy mind, which he had always felt was a hindrance to his meditation practice, was actually not the problem. He could now just *watch* the busy mind, orbiting from the space of mindfulness. Surely this was not all there could be, orbiting around his experiences? How could he possibly achieve anything in life simply by watching what was happening in his life?

He had always enjoyed the process and feeling of improvement. He had a 'growth mindset,' regularly enjoying new challenges and learning from them. How can you achieve a goal without striving hard, he wondered? He posed this to the online community, which started an interesting and lively discussion with a number of people of what seemed to work for them and what didn't.

Through the forum, he came across a phrase called Right Effort, one of the eight spokes of the Noble Eightfold Path that the Buddha taught. This set of eight was a framework that described the path that led out of suffering. Peter still didn't know what to make of the Four Noble Truths, but the fourth truth was this Noble Eightfold Path and he thought Right Effort was a good place to start exploring things.

What is Right Effort? He came across a description of a quadrant system that systematised Right Effort. The system comprised the effort to:

- Prevent unskilful or unwholesome qualities, especially greed, anger, and ignorance, from arising.
- Extinguish unskilful or unwholesome qualities that already have arisen.
- Cultivate skilful or wholesome qualities, especially generosity, loving-kindness, and wisdom.
- Strengthen skilful or wholesome qualities that have already arisen.

This made intuitive sense to Peter, who enjoyed working within classification systems. He thought the list for each of these categories would be too long and decided he could double down on one thing at a time, for each category. In his case, he would need to somehow:

- Prevent greed from arising.
- Extinguish his anxiety.
- Cultivate loving-kindness.
- Strengthen his quality of determination.

He didn't know where to start when he looked at the list. He let this percolate in his mind as he carried on with the rest of his day. Through this practice of mindfulness, he was now trusting the process to unfold the way it needed to. His habit of trying to figure things out (through attention) was still there, but he was more accepting of allowing 'the other part of his brain' (awareness) to come up with solutions.

Sure enough, one day while he was in the shower, the solution presented itself. If he tackled the list in the *reverse order*, everything made sense. In order to strengthen his already strong determination, he would use this quality in the exploration of Right Effort.

Peter knew he tended to strive too hard when he set his mind on something. The word 'effort' in Right Effort somehow seemed to trigger his habit of over-exerting himself. He had clearly defined what he wanted to achieve, but how could he change the habit of 'over-efforting'? Surely that would negate the 'right' part of Right Effort?

The paradox was too much, once again, for his conceptual brain. He decided to let it be and allow his awareness to do its thing of coming up with creative solutions to problems. This seemed the only sensible option for the moment.

Peter woke up the next morning with the solution. His goals were to increase his determination and loving-kindness whilst decreasing his anxiety and greed. He had decided to work on one thing at a time, starting with determination. Just setting this intention and trusting the process was enough for his awareness to take over and work with his already well-established determination to come up with this solution. How amazing was that!

The solution came in the image of a compass. If his next goal was to increase his loving-kindness, all he needed was a 'loving-kindness compass.' Anytime during the day, he could check to see if his compass was pointing towards loving-kindness, was slightly askew, or even pointing in the opposite direction. His job would simply be to turn himself towards his intended goal of loving-kindness.

When he was interacting with his partner and was triggered by something she had said or done, he would previously have shut down and ceased communication with her for long periods of time. He knew this was not a good pattern of behaviour, for this often sent his partner down a more negative spiral that he would eventually need to help her out of.

When they next had an argument, Peter kept his 'loving-kindness compass' firmly in view. Whenever he was about to say something out of anger, hurt, or sadness, he decided to refrain from this because it was not in the service of cultivating loving-kindness. He would instead notice his strong reaction, appreciate that he had a brief reprieve in the orbit of awareness, and take things down a notch by consciously relaxing his body, taking a few deeper breaths, or even excusing himself to go to the bathroom to allow more time and space to do this.

Life became softer, calmer, and more pleasant through this practice. When he set himself to cultivate more loving-kindness, he regularly checked his compass to ensure every word and action he took was in this direction. He would spend entire days, and even weeks, engaging in this gentle and wonderful practice of loving-kindness.

If he read something terrible about the state of the world in the news, instead of reacting in anger like he normally did, he clearly started seeing how his anger served no purpose but to harm himself and the people around him who didn't enjoy his tirades at these times. He did not come up with useful solutions to the injustice he saw through these bouts of fury, so why continue them? Why not try to find a different way of being, and in so doing, open himself to allowing real solutions to emerge? Why not continue to trust the process of awareness to a larger extent?

So when he found himself furious at yet another issue, he chose to send himself loving-kindness. This was sometimes difficult, so he started by forgiving himself for not being able to. He forgave himself for not seeing clearly and being so angry unnecessarily, and thereby harming the well-being of himself and his partner. He forgave the misguided people who were involved in perpetrating the injustice. His practice of forgiveness naturally extended to all the people around him, past and present. It extended to his mother for having made his life so complicated, to his neighbour who played loud music over the weekend, to his boss for being unreasonable.

The practice of forgiveness seemed to change his experiences in surprisingly empowering ways. Things that normally would have infuriated him now slid off him like water off a duck's back. This didn't mean they no longer mattered to him, though. To the contrary, Peter found that he had better clarity and could now separate the wheat from the chaff.

Instead of feeling powerless in the face of injustice or engaging in what used to be his favourite hobby of 'solving the world's problems' in one tirade, he now found that remembering to check his 'loving-kindness compass,' and course correcting as appropriate, kept him on track to continue to live according to his true values.

Peter also kept his 'anxiety compass' at hand throughout his days. Whether he was at home preparing a meal, at work with his colleagues, going for a stroll, or walking through the supermarket, he kept his eye on his 'anxiety compass' to ensure he was always facing the direction of less anxiety and more calm.

When his anxiety was too high, he was now able to naturally reduce it at will. 'Taking things down a notch' was now such an automatic process for him that he wondered how he could ever have lived without this skill. When his anxiety was not too high, he let it rest in the space of awareness and became interested in the seemingly endless interconnections of what he had once assumed to be an isolated experience.

He came to see how some of the habits of his mind were related to his regular experience of anxiety. These included his tendency towards perfectionism that seemed to be related to constant expectations of excellence and a habit of striving too hard. Similarly, his tendency to always want to fix things led to feelings of frustration whenever he felt he could not fix them quickly enough.

Whenever he compared himself to others, to what he had previously been able to do, or to what he had set as his aim but not yet achieved, his anxiety also seemed to increase. Peter came to see that expectation was the discrepancy between what is *currently* happening and what he *wanted* to happen, and whenever expectation was there, he experienced anxiety.

He saw that the arising of greed was also related to expectation. When there was more greed, it seemed to be related to a greater discrepancy between what he wanted and what was actually present. This discrepancy was associated with a resistance in his mind to the reality of the moment.

Peter clearly saw that his stress and anxiety was related to this resistance to what was truly happening in the moment. The question arose again: now that I am orbiting in the awareness of this realisation, what next? Is this all this practice of mindfulness is about? He posed the question to his teacher in the next group mentoring session.

The teacher's answer:

What you have described is an essential first step. But the practice does not stop here. Instead of drowning in your stress and anxiety, you have now learnt to surf the waves of life through mindfulness. But you are not trying to power that surfboard; all you need to do is steer it appropriately.

So the first step in this process is to learn to not drown and instead hop onto the board—in other words, take things down a notch. The next step is to actually surf. In other words, the next step involves your power of choice when you are in the orbit of awareness.

The point of this practice is to give you the reprieve of the space of awareness in order to make appropriate choices of where to put your attention. Once you are aware of, for example, something that is causing you anger, is it more beneficial to keep thinking about the situation (and thereby increase your anger), or would you like to exercise the choice to direct your attention towards something that will reduce it?

This is always your choice. Your habits will determine your choice made at a more unconscious level. Your growing mindfulness will allow you to choose more consciously. It doesn't matter if you are aware of kindness or anger, joy or sadness, equanimity or agitation, certainty or confusion. In each moment you are aware that the feelings or mind states have arisen, you have a choice to continue in the habitual trajectory or forge a different path. This path allows you to re-chart the course of your life, and you do this more consciously and deliberately when you have the perspective of strong mindfulness.

Choice. Who would have thought that a practice that was seemingly so passive was actually about increasing our choices to make more appropriate decisions in life? Peter considered this. No, it was not actually passive at all. The practice was really about being *receptive*. In his pursuit of improvement, Peter had only learnt how to progress through active and forceful striving. This new practice was different because it taught him how to cultivate receptive awareness. The only effort he needed to make was to remember to positively reinforce awareness whenever it was present. With time and consistency, this automatically culminated into the new skill of effortless effort.

How liberating this was! Tuning into awareness was the only thing Peter needed to do. Once he was more conscious of what was occurring, he could then exercise his power of choice to take action in the most beneficial direction.

CHAPTER 5
WHAT FIRES TOGETHER WIRES TOGETHER

T hings were starting to sail smoothly now. Peter felt the freedom of sailing in open waters, with the wind in his hair and his eye on the compass. He didn't need to power the boat; his only job was to steer the ship of his life. How liberating!

He continued his exploration into greed, for he had always found this extremely challenging. He somehow knew that his relationship with food, with progress in meditation, with wanting to improve himself, with everything, was often tinged with a sense of a strong desire for what was not present, and this caused him a lot of grief. This desire sometimes came in the form of a very visceral lurch that cantankerously said in his head, 'I want! I want!' There was no taming it.

Peter felt somewhat ashamed to have this. It felt ugly to him; unbecoming of the sort of person he had held himself to be. As he struggled with this, he continued with the video lessons. There was a lady who had asked about why it was so important to smile in appreciation when she noticed her tendency towards perfectionism. Perfectionism was the bane of her existence! Why should she smile at it?

The teacher said:

The best way our brains work to form new habits is through positive reinforcement. Punishments don't work as effectively as positive reinforcement. Thirty years ago, I was a piano teacher. My aim with all my students was not to make them practise, it was to help them enjoy playing the piano. If my students left my studio singing, skipping, and smiling, I knew that was a good lesson.

Why? Because I knew that because they were happy during the lesson, a positive association with playing the piano had been formed. Dopamine, endorphins and serotonin were coursing through their brains and they were much more likely to want this experience again ... and therefore, practise more (I was also doing a masters in cognitive science at the time and a bit of a neuro-geek trying to hack the brain in different ways).

When you smile in appreciation of the awareness when it has noticed anything (yes, including the fact that you have a tendency towards perfectionism), you are reinforcing the awareness. I'm not suggesting you smile in appreciation of the thing that is causing you grief; I am suggesting that you smile at the recognition of this.

The lady responded that she has always been aware of this, and that her experience was that her perfectionism always took over. She always ended up more anxious, agitated and frustrated when confronted with a task that she was not able to do.

The teacher continued:

Our objective is to cultivate more awareness. Whether you are wishing to stress a little less, cultivate deep states of meditation, or eliminate stress and suffering entirely from your life, awareness is the key.

If you notice that your agitation and frustration has escalated, consciously relax your body, and take it down a notch. Now, this is the important part I am emphasising here: smile to yourself for a job well done! This encourages your brain to continue to be aware.

When most people notice their frustration has escalated, they get annoyed and frustrated at themselves. This is basically saying to your brain: 'I don't want to be aware anymore, because I don't like being frustrated.' So the neural pathways associated with awareness don't get reinforced.

Smile in appreciation of the awareness and enjoy that moment of reprieve when you are temporarily not stuck in the stickiness of the frustration. You are basically making a choice to do this instead of falling straight back into the frustration. From this vantage, you have another choice now: get sucked back into the frustration, continue to feel the appreciation, or choose to direct your attention to something entirely different that may be more beneficial for you.

There was another question about someone having difficulties sticking to the diligence of committing to this practice each day.

Peter found the teacher's response surprising:

I emphasise appreciation and gratitude because softening into this way of being feels nice and is empowering. I started this course encouraging all of you to dedicate at least ten minutes each day to develop your seated practice, and regular moments during the day to cultivate mindfulness in daily life.

If you managed to do this, great. Enjoy the feeling of succeeding in sticking to your commitment. If you didn't, forgive yourself. It's absolutely alright. It's not the end of the world. Tomorrow is a new day.

The thing is, learning frequently happens by simply showing up. Set an alarm on your phone to meditate, and show up. When you show up, start by smiling and thanking yourself for doing what you set out to do. Then sit there and enjoy being present to yourself. Show up for yourself, in whatever state you are in. Be present to you in those ten minutes. Lean into an appreciation of the fact that you can be aware and see how enjoyable this can be.

Life can really be quite delightful. Can you taste it?

Peter was really enjoying the video lessons. Even though the videos were recorded from a course that had occurred in the past, he had gotten to know the voices and characteristics of each of the people who asked questions and enjoyed the responses from the teacher. He frequently re-listened to the short instructions and guided meditations, and was surprised at how he seemed to understand the same instructions in different ways.

Peter enjoyed the live group mentoring sessions where he could ask questions, be guided in the subtleties of his actual practice, and listen to advice to other students. He also came to really appreciate his fellow meditators who formed the online community. They had lively discussions on various topics, and Peter felt safe to share thoughts and ideas in this space.

He reflected on this fact. Peter had always felt like an outlier in the world. He was smarter than the other kids at school and always bullied for that. As a young child, he had retreated into the world of books and computers, and never really liked the idea of interacting with groups. He was most definitely an introvert. Yet, he was comfortable in this Collective Wisdom community. What was that, he wondered?

He smiled at himself when the thought arose: Why not pose that question to the community? He did, and was surprised at the number of people who responded to say that they felt the same way. They had always shied away from group-work, they said. Some, in fact, said they even tended to avoid interacting with people in general, yet were discussing the most intimate reflections of their mind with total strangers in this community.

The teacher piped into the conversation:

It's not at all surprising, you know. We are, after all, meditators! We are drawn to this strange and wonderful practice of training the mind, introspection, and self-inquiry. We are a minority in the world, and this is the exact reason why I set up this community.

I know it is not obvious when I am mentoring you in the groups, because I talk for the entire hour and a half; but I normally don't talk a lot. When you ask a question and I feel I can help, the response seems to have a life of its own. But this is not my natural state of being. I am actually a very quiet person. I enjoy the company of other people, but I enjoy the company of myself even more. So apart from when I am in front of the camera talking to you, or doing physical activities with others, I can usually be found working alone in front of my computer, reading, meditating, immersed in practising the guitar or piano, or spending quiet time with my husband.

I set up this platform because I saw that there are many meditators out there who would benefit from community—what is known in Buddhism as a saṅgha. We go on meditation retreats in silence, experience profound changes in solitude, and only very occasionally interact with teachers and our fellow students. Most of our family members don't have a clue about this very important aspect of our lives. We start to take the teachings of being 'an island unto yourself' a little too literally.

This teaching is meant to be about being a refuge for yourself. It's not about believing that you are an actual island, separated from other islands of the world. In fact, I once came across an idea that in most cultures, when someone says the word 'islands,' people think of several solitary pieces of land separated by water. But in one culture (I don't remember which one), the word 'islands' conjures up the feel of a body of water that includes the pieces of land. Do you see the difference?

The perspective is a figure-ground shift. We feel a sense of disconnection because we perceive we are individual nodes of a network. We are not; we are the network. You may conceptually understand the notion of a network, but do you still see yourself as a separate node in the whole system? Do you sometimes compare yourself to other nodes in the system, saying they are not pulling their weight, or they are not doing things correctly? Do you continue to have an 'us and them' mentality?

The reality is, we are the network; we are not just part of it. The extent to which we can really experience this is the extent we can free our mind to the real possibilities of our marvellous existence.

Peter paused as he let this sink into his being. We are the network. We are the ocean. There is no separation. He was reminded of a talk he had watched by the late Vietnamese Zen monk, Thich Nhat Hanh, who was talking about interbeing. We are not you and me. We are all inextricably connected.

He remembered the monk's gentle, kind voice as he gave

this example. If you are hammering a nail, with the right hand holding the hammer and the left hand the nail, and the right hand accidentally hits the left hand, what happens? Does the left hand get angry and shout at the right hand for being careless, or for doing that on purpose? Does the right hand get offended and hurt, and defend itself and continue the argument? No. The right hand does what is most natural; it picks up the throbbing left hand and holds it until the pain eases. It doesn't believe it is separate from the other hand.

This is what compassion is really about. In understanding that there is no separation, the natural response in the face of another's suffering is care.

Peter decided to start exploring the experiences of his life and world around him from this perspective. It was easy to slide back into the habit of dichotomies, in looking at things from a 'us and them' perspective, but he resolved to notice what that felt like when this happened.

He remembered another statement by Thich Nhat Hanh that had always puzzled him. The statement said something about the 'delusion of inferiority, superiority, and equality.' He understood, at least conceptually, that the sense of inferiority can be delusional. He had suffered from imposter syndrome for much of his life, and although he knew that he was good at what he did, he did intermittently feel like a bit of a fraud.

He also understood the delusion of superiority. He certainly saw that in other people. Peter wondered if he sometimes suffered from that as well. When he felt bad about himself, didn't he sometimes double down on stating his achievements, and rely on his intellect to put others down? Didn't he sometimes demonstrate the delusion of superiority?

And then there was the delusion of equality. This statement never made sense to him, but now, as he considered that he was the ocean, not just a small, separate part of it, any sense of comparison was meaningless. 'It is all a delusion!' he thought. 'But how easy it is to get caught up in this delusion over and over again.'

Peter explored this each time the sense 'I' formed, separate from the rest of the world. He noticed that whenever this happened, he felt a visceral sense of congealment in his body. How fascinating! Could this congealment be related to the ego that one loses when people talk about being on the spiritual path? He felt imprisoned by the sense of separation and disconnection every time it was present.

Peter knew this was just the beginning. There was so much more he wanted to learn.

PART THREE
FREEDOM FROM SUFFERING

Many people seek to alleviate their stress and suffering in order to move through their lives with more ease. Part Two of this book describes practices that can be mastered within three months, if applied with diligence. If maintained thereafter, practitioners can continue to strengthen their new habit of inclining their mind towards ease and well-being.

There are those among us who are called, for some inextricable reason, to a deeper spiritual pursuit. Part Three of this book describes some practices I feel form part of the 5 sets of missing ingredients to awakening, as described in Part One, from a Buddhist perspective.

The practices in this part of the book do not follow a linear progression. Although they necessarily need to be taught and sometimes practised one at a time, they invariably coalesce to form a singular practice of life, in service of flowing in tune with the *Dhamma*.

The first chapter of this section about The Unconscious Ascetic describes the subtle interplay between suffering and seeking in an exploration of the First Noble Truth. The next chapter about awareness and alignment discusses the Fourth Noble Truth in a slightly re-envisioned Noble Eight-fold Path, with emphasis on what I frequently see students miss in the actual application of Walking the Path of what the Buddha taught.

'The Devil is in the Detail' discusses more nuances of the Noble Eightfold Path and emphasises a healthy balance between spiritual urgency and equanimity. Through under-standing 'The Singular Cause of Your Suffering,' the following chapter provides a compass for this entire path as it explores The Second Noble Truth. Finally, the last chapter explores the Third Noble Truth, the reality of Freeing Our Mind from stress and suffering, permanently.

I wrote this book after publishing the first draft of the prologue online, asking readers if they would be interested in reading a book such as this, and if they had any specific questions they wanted me to address. Over 150 readers responded with hundreds of questions. I have attempted to address every one of these questions through this book. I have furnished the answers with practical examples of my own and students' experiences and understandings in order to inspire others to practise and realise the reality of the Third Noble Truth, the end of suffering.

With respect and humility, here is Part Three of the book.

CHAPTER 1
THE UNCONSCIOUS ASCETIC

It was my third meditation retreat in the Goenka tradition. I had found the other two retreats to be life-changing, and had developed a different relationship with myself and my body through this process.

I was lying in my tent gasping for air. I was calm as I accepted my fate. The reality of *anicca*, impermanence of life, had permeated my being. If I were to die right now, I would be at peace. I had spent the entire retreat watching a searing pain in my mouth and now, in the middle of the night, I was suffering from an asthma attack.

I continued to lie there quietly. I did not wish to disturb the other retreatants. I continued putting my attention to scanning my body, watching the dissolution of the sensations.

When the retreat ended, I realised that the pain in my mouth that I had been watching had increased. Oh yes! I now remembered that I had been watching a toothache in addition to having difficulties breathing! I made an appointment with my dentist that week and chatted with him in our usual way. When I finally got to opening my mouth and letting him look at my teeth, he gasped.

'Are you in a lot of pain?'

'Yeah, a fair bit of pain.'

'How long has this been going on for?'

'About ten days.'

He was horrified. I had apparently been watching a tooth abscess grow over ten days, and there was no option now but to remove the tooth after a course of antibiotics. I left this to my dentist's capable hands and was in no pain before long.

This got me thinking. I thought I was practising the *Dhamma* through changing my relationship with pain, but maybe there was something I was missing. Surely this path is not just about *blindly* watching pain? I recalled my childhood, when I thought I would make the greatest spy. My ability to tolerate pain was such that I knew I would never give away any secrets if caught by the enemy.

I remembered going to the dentist as a child and asking him not to inject me with local anaesthesia before drilling into my teeth. I recalled dozens of other instances where I had deliberately put myself in situations of disregard for my body. Had I somehow conflated self-mortification with the Buddhist path to liberation?

I decided to read through stories of the Buddha. Since attending retreats in this tradition, I had stopped reading anything to do with this, and had instead solely engaged in the practice as had been directed. Maybe it was time to go to the source of these teachings now.

It soon became clear to me that I was not alone in the pursuit of self-mortification. The Buddha himself had engaged in ascetic practices for a period of time, where he deprived himself of food and water in his quest for enlightenment. It was only when he realised the Middle Way that he awakened to the reality of our existence.

I wondered if I had fallen down the same trap. The Buddha had consciously chosen to explore the path of the ascetics. I, on the other hand, had apparently been an unconscious ascetic all of my life.

What I had assumed was equanimity, an even-tempered state of being, was often ambivalence on an unconscious level. It is often said that indifference is the near-enemy of equanimity, but I came to see that in my case, I had mistaken an unconscious ambivalence about myself for equanimity. It was as if I cared and did not care about my well-being.

I have since come across many students who have this same misguided perception. There is a certain amount of self-loathing mixed into things, and this unconscious ambivalence results in a far more pernicious state of being.

In my case, there seemed to be an unconscious disregard for myself, and the suffering of my body, which prevented the practice of many essential aspects of this path. Before even beginning to experience equanimity, I needed to first experience loving-kindness for myself. At that time, that was as foreign for me as living on Neptune!

I grew to understand that it was not possible to experience loving-kindness for myself because I was not even acknowledging the truth of my own suffering. I was seeking the end of suffering, but frequently not actually aware *that* I was suffering. Denying the existence of suffering was no way to transcend it! Once I came to recognise this fact, I realised that the practice I really needed to engage in was one of self-compassion. It took me a lot of time, and tears, to truly engage in this practice, but once I experienced this in reality, rather than merely conceptually, it totally transformed my relationship with myself. Thereafter, this also naturally changed my relationships with all the people around me.

I have since met many students who also very often deny they are suffering in any way whatsoever. If you fall into this category, I would encourage you to explore this question: if the Buddhist path to awakening is about the end of suffering, then what are you practising to attain?

Having spoken to many people about this, I see that sometimes it's the word 'suffering' that they react to. They reflect on what they experience and compare it to some notion of what they think 'real suffering' is, and decide that their life circumstances are merely a mild version of a padded hell, which somehow does not qualify them to be placed in this category. It is as if they compare themselves to what other people are experiencing in life and think that they don't deserve to be able to call their experience 'suffering.'

This is unacknowledged suffering.

Suffering is suffering. There is stress in life. There is fear, loss, grief and change in life that naturally results in suffering. Suffering is not about the external circumstances you find yourself in; it is about your mental state of being. If there is any sense of unsatisfactoriness in your experience of life, this is what *dukkha* is. If you don't like the word 'suffering,' substitute it with something more palatable for you. But the end result is this: unless you acknowledge that there is unsatisfactoriness in your existence, it makes no sense to try to transcend it. And spiritual awakening *is* about transcending this.

This path is about non-resistance. It is not about denying the existence of the reality of *dukkha*. Understanding the reality of the suffering is as essential on this path as is seeking a way out of it. This is the stark reality of the first Noble Truth.

A little tip to help you recognise when there may be unacknowledged suffering is when there is any sense of conflict in your mind. This usually comes when you have dichotomised things conceptually into 'right' and 'wrong.' Ideas, views and opinions can be wonderful things, but they can also be extremely pernicious when they are so lodged in your unconscious that you are unable to perceive things in any other way.

One example that is particularly prevalent in the spiritual world relates to money. There is an idea, borne of the understanding that greed is a dangerous 'poison' that obstructs the spiritual path, that *any* materiality is incompatible with spirituality. The dichotomy that is set up through this idea has some unfortunate consequences.

All too often, I see excellent *Dhamma* teachers live in poverty. This is particularly true for lay, female *Dhamma* teachers, but many nuns in the world suffer the same fate of not having sufficient food, medicine, and shelter to support themselves. If the teachers live in countries where there is no provision of healthcare, they often suffer greatly when their health is compromised.

I see this as a conflation of and clinging to ideas. The practice of *dāna*, or generosity and non-greed, is essential on the spiritual path. Generosity is the opening of the heart to include the well-being of ourselves and others in one's thoughts, speech, and action. Poverty is not a virtue; non-greed and generosity are. If we are to follow this path to awakening, we really need to be more conscious in our practice of generosity in our thoughts and deeds. Note this has nothing whatsoever to do with accepting money in exchange for teaching or mentoring. Watch out for the tendency to criticise others (*dosa*) if they don't conform to your notion of what is 'spiritual.' Let go of the clinging to ideas, particularly if you believe them to be absolute truths.

Here is another example. Your body is a gift from the universe. You are responsible for its care. To deliberately starve yourself because of a peculiar concept of 'spirituality' is an offence to nature. On the other extreme, to engage in gluttony is equally offensive. Treat your own body with both generosity and non-greed. Take care of it as you would take care of a loved one.

As a psychotherapist and a meditation teacher, people often ask me about my view on the relationship between psychotherapy and this path to awakening. I think they are both important. Not everyone was brought up in an optimal environment. Childhood experiences form the bedrock of the psyche of a person. Dysfunctional family dynamics, trauma, and loss are some of the multitudes of experiences that can detrimentally affect a person's ability to cope with the vicissitudes of life.

This is particularly so in the relational realm. Psychotherapy can help in many ways, and none more so than allowing a person who has only experienced dysfunctional relational patterns in the past to open to the reality of healthy, trusting, and loving relationships. Through a healthy, intimate relationship with the client, the therapist can form a bond that models a type of relationship never experienced before, thereby paving the way for more similarly healthy relationships thereafter.

I feel that the ability to trust is essential prior to embarking on this spiritual path. This is because one can encounter many strange and unusual phenomena, and without the support and guidance of a trusted mentor or teacher it is very easy to get lost along the journey. I can only help people who acknowledge they are suffering, are seeking my help, and are able to trust me in being able to support them. If you have difficulties in trusting others, you will need to overcome this in order to progress along the path. Remember that even the Buddha had teachers who guided him along his journey to awakening.

There is no room for spiritual bypassing on this path. Any time people do this, it will inevitably come back to bite them. Everything that arises in your mind *is* this path, so if you need a therapist to help you with it, go to a therapist. If you need a meditation mentor, find one. Try not to dichotomise things into *Dhamma* versus psychotherapy. Everything in life is the *Dhamma*. We are looking to understand and eliminate suffering, and any insight into and support for this helps.

When people reach the higher stages of this path, it may well be true that the word 'suffering' really does not apply to their experience. Yet, the unsatisfactoriness of *dukkha* is still present. Connect to the reality of *dukkha*, explore it, and seek to understand the full extent of this. This is the only way to full awakening.

In the later paths of this practice, *dukkha* may be more subtle, but it is still invariably there. At times, slight annoyance may rear its head. Or there may be subtle wanting, perhaps no longer of material possessions, but possibly of spiritual attainments. Sometimes, these manifest as a lot more than subtle desire, and result in putting too much effort into the pursuit of your aims. And always be on the lookout for the tendency to dichotomise the world. This subtle sense of 'I am right and you are wrong' pervades right through to the total dissolution of the ego.

One way to explore these subtler forms of *dukkha* is to notice little 'catches' in your experience of life. If you imagine running your hand along some smooth, shiny silk, if there was a slight tag in your skin, it would 'catch' the silk and prevent the smooth gliding of your flow in life. These 'catches' can be seen as subtle expressions of *dukkha*, your resistance to life, and can serve as opportunities to explore, learn from, and understand your experiences in a deeper way.

Post-awakening, the body can still be stressed. There may be no adverse reactions from the mind as a consequence of pain, but it is essential to remember this reality. I remember a conversation I had with Culadasa, the author of *The Mind Illuminated*, about a year prior to his passing. He told me a story of a time he had spent at the hospital emergency department. He had metastatic cancer and was in more severe pain than usual.

The nurses asked him what the level of his pain was, to which he replied, 'It's tolerable.' The hospital staff left him lying there for hours as a result. Then it occurred to him that their questioning was part of the triaging system and that even though he could tolerate the pain, that was not the point of the exercise. Just because there was no stress in the mind did not mean that the stress in the body had to be tolerated! The next time they asked about his level of pain, he gave them an appropriate number that sent him straight to the operation room.

I am constantly on the lookout for the signs of stress in the body. There may be no concomitant mental stress but deeply ingrained patterns can still play a large role in the mind and prevent skilful actions.

This is the only mind and body we have. We need to take care to keep the stress levels down at all times. The practices of Part Two remain as important as before, to be engaged in whenever appropriate.

CHAPTER 2
WALKING THE PATH

This practice necessarily starts with the cultivation of awareness, irrespective of the object of meditation. As I frequently say to my students who are in this initial stage of developing stronger awareness, 'Awareness doesn't care what it is aware of; it is only you who does.' What I mean by this is that sometimes students get fixated on the fact that they have noticed certain not-so-healthy habitual patterns of mind, that they get caught up in the attempt to fix things before cultivating sufficient awareness for wisdom to arise.

At this stage of the practice, it is essential that they continue to cultivate the strength of their awareness through the positive reinforcement of joy and appreciation, as discussed in Part Two of this book. There comes a time, though, that the pure cultivation of awareness in and of itself needs direction. This is the path of wisdom, and it is here that awareness alone is not enough.

Alignment with the *Dhamma* is an essential next stage of practice. Many Buddhist practitioners have come across the

Noble Eightfold Path but don't know how to apply it, in a practical way, to their lives. Mindfulness all the time allows insights to unfold throughout one's daily life, and the Noble Eightfold Path is a perfect framework that provides the conditions for insights to arise.

Imagine a wheel as symbolic of your life (It's a popular enough metaphor). A long time ago, wheels were solid wooden rotating disks. Most people's lives are like these heavy, bulky wheels—before spokes came along! You are carrying extra weight and not knowing any better.

The innovation of spokes led to the swifter movement of wheels. The *Dharmachakra* wheel uses spokes to represent different aspects of teachings. Traditionally, the Eightfold Path was represented by eight spokes.

However, when I teach this Noble Eightfold Path as a clear way out of suffering, I teach all these eight principles condensed into five. And there are some very practical and pertinent reasons for doing this.

In the Buddha's time, people were accustomed to memorising. These days, how many of us can remember even a mobile phone number?

I try to empower students to recall principles in their daily practice. For this reason, I created the acronym SPOKE, which condenses the Eightfold Path into five!

S - Stabilising your attention.

P - Prioritising your actions.

O - Opening your awareness.

K - Kindling your understanding.

E - Expanding your world.

As a meditation teacher and spiritual life coach, I find there is one crucial skill in achieving success: having sufficient alignment in life to have a clear path for your plan of action. Meditators often underestimate the need for clear aims to help bring alignment into their lives.

Each of the five spokes is therefore written with a clear aim in mind. Each is also stated in the present continuous of '~ing' to encapsulate the continual process of development.

All spokes balance each other out for optimal strength, form, and function. Gradually, by refining your practice one rotation at a time, you will arrive at your destination. There will be bumps in the road as well as ups and downs but life's journey, like all journeys, is hardly ever straight and easy.

I generally teach this system one spoke at a time. But, as you progress, it's easy to experience the synergy and the deepening of awareness, and the unfolding of awakening.

I will now map these five spokes to the Noble Eightfold Path in a way that maintains the integrity of what the Buddha taught.

SPOKE 1 - STABILISING YOUR ATTENTION

Stabilising your attention refers to *sammā-samādhi* (right concentration). Since 'concentration' leads to a host of confusions in English, I prefer instead to use 'attention,' which describes the way you attend to things, rather than the result.

The cultivation of attention leads to a mind stable enough to tolerate the vicissitudes of life. I teach Culadasa's Ten Stage method, which is based on Asanga's elephant path, as meticulously spelt out in his book, *The Mind Illuminated*.

This book begins with Stage One, setting up the foundations to Establishing the Practice, and progresses with detailed instructions of the path and how to work with the various issues of distraction, dullness, and purifications. Gems of wisdom are scattered throughout the book, which together open astute readers to the portals of awakening. As Culadasa used to say, 'Awakening is an accident, and developing the ten stages of *samatha* makes you more accident-prone.'

The ten stages take students through three different versions of the eight *jhānas*, bypassing the controversies of *sutta* versus *visuddhimagga jhānas* by including both. The book starts with cultivating awareness, then develops attention through the stages, and ends in pure awareness (or technically, when the scope of attention expands to the field of awareness) through more advanced practices such as the Tibetan Dzogchen practice of mahāmudrā.

Stabilising your attention is essential for developing a mind that is equanimous and calm. Aligning with this aim is part of walking the Noble Eightfold Path.

SPOKE 2 - PRIORITISING YOUR ACTIONS

Prioritising your actions is an amalgamation of three axioms of the Eightfold Path. These are *sammā-vācā* (right speech), *sammā-kammanta* (right action), and *sammā-ājīva* (right livelihood).

Right Speech encompasses a five-fold process of speaking in a truthful, beneficial, timely, pleasant, and kindful way. This list of five is enough to keep your practice true to this path, irrespective of wherever you are along the journey. While many people know the first tenet of speaking in a truthful manner, how many ensure their speech is always beneficial, timely, pleasant, and imbued with loving-kindness?

Right Action in the basic sense means abstaining from

killing, stealing, and sexual misconduct. More fundamentally, it refers to the tenet of ahimsa, non-violence. Prior to taking any action, reflect on it and ask yourself if this action may lead to harm to yourself or others.

In a similar way, Right Livelihood refers to engaging in work that is beneficial, rather than harmful, to yourself and others.

When the first two axioms of Right Speech and Right Action align, this congruence, or lack of internal conflict, quickly unburdens the mind of stress and needless suffering. In turn, this then culminates in right living.

SPOKE 3 - OPENING YOUR AWARENESS

Opening your awareness refers to *sammā-sati* (right mindfulness). Again, due to different definitions of 'mindfulness' that are prevalent, I prefer to use the word 'awareness.'

Meditation is more than focused attention on a particular object. Opening your awareness goes beyond to encompass the arising and passing away of phenomena and the dependent arisings of our existence.

In a simple example from Part Two of this book, in expanded or meta awareness, you develop the ability to tune into the arising of stress and anxiety as it manifests. This allows you to then 'nip it in the bud' and be proactive in reducing the stress rather than let it escalate out of control.

Opening your awareness to the Noble Eightfold Path allows you to live your life in congruence with, providing the groundwork for the ripening of awakening. You first familiarise yourself with this framework, as a whole or in part. Then you keep this in mind throughout your day, continuing to align your thoughts, speech, and action in congruence with it. Only then are you walking the path.

Sayadaw U Tejaniya's teachings of engaging in the practice of mindfulness in daily life provides a perfect framework for the cultivation of continuous awareness. Posing the simple questions, 'What is happening now? What am I aware of?' helps kick-start the process. The fact is, we are aware every moment we are conscious. We are aware from the moment we wake up until the moment we fall asleep. We are training to remain connected with this awareness that is always present.

Far too many words have been written about this already. Just pause for a while and start the practice now. Can you recognise the fact that you are already aware? Can you rest in this awareness? Can you be content that you have just connected with the awareness, and put a smile on your face in appreciation of this?

SPOKE 4 - KINDLING YOUR UNDERSTANDING

Kindling your understanding refers to *sammā-diṭṭhi* (right understanding or view).

Right understanding isn't a question of reading or listening to *Dhamma* books and talks, and understanding things conceptually. It is a gradual and layered process of slowly building upon truthful information, applying it in daily life, and reaping the fruits of your own experience. With each iteration, deeper understanding can be kindled until this culminates into true insights.

Your understanding of the Noble Eightfold Path may be cursory at the moment. Or you may have studied this extensively. Either way, this is only starting to scratch the surface of *sammā-diṭṭhi*. Ask yourself: do you tend to be attached to certain views or ways of being in the world? Is there any sense of comparison, or sense of 'My way is better than your way' or 'Your way of looking at things is wrong and mine is right? This is wrong view (*micchā diṭṭhi*).

Wrong view is pernicious. The trouble with conceptualisation is that our ideas are sticky. Once we believe something is true, it clouds our perception, and this makes it very difficult to see the other side.

Let me give you an example of a *Dhamma* teacher, but you can substitute this for your own situation.

The challenge of accepting the role of a *Dhamma* teacher is the incredible responsibility involved. People's spiritual lives are at stake! As a consequence, you take the role very seriously and learn in every possible way to be up to the task. As you become more experienced in this, it is easy to unconsciously start forming certain ideas of how best to teach people. If another teacher has a different opinion (based invariably on their different experience), how much do you tend to cling to your own ideas? Do you tend to find a group of other like-minded teachers to confirm your views? To what extent do you live in an echo-chamber of your views?

A good way to continue to explore *sammā-diṭṭhi* is to notice your reaction to a conflicting view and bring this to your explorations in meditation. Is there clinging to a certain way of thinking about things? Is there an expectation of conformity or agreement? Is there a sense of an absolute right in the issue? Any opinion is of the mundane realm. *Sammā-diṭṭhi* refers to an alignment with the *Dhamma*, where one ultimately meets others in a space of coherence and unity. This is an experience well beyond words and concepts which can only be felt as an insight in the flow of practice.

Another good thing to do is to always come from what I call the 'I don't know mind.' This feels to me like the experiential aspect of the Zen beginner's mind, without any conceptual frameworks. I am constantly trying to find new ways to discover how I can stop assuming I know the intentions of others, and use every interaction to learn more about my own possible subtle, conflicting intentions.

I am fortunate that I love learning, so every interaction with anyone is an opportunity for me to learn. On the one hand I usually learn something from the person directly and on the other hand I often learn something from our interaction itself; how it unfolds, where we run into problems and how to improve our communication. So, even from a discussion about a topic on which we completely disagree, valuable lessons can be learnt.

If you want to align with the *Dhamma*, live life from this space of a beginner's mind. In the words of Thich Nhat Hanh, watch out for 'the delusion of inferiority, the delusion of superiority, and the delusion of equality.'

SPOKE 5 - EXPANDING YOUR WORLD

Expanding your world refers to *sammā-vāyāma* (right effort), and *sammā-saṅkappa* (right intention).

Right Effort starts with recognising beneficial qualities you possess, and those that you don't. Likewise, detrimental (non-beneficial) qualities you have, and those you don't. The idea here is twofold. One is to *strengthen* beneficial qualities you possess and *cultivate* those you don't. Likewise, to *abandon* detrimental ones and *prevent* manifesting those you don't possess.

Beneficial qualities, such as the Ten Perfections (*pāramī*), include generosity, non-violence, kindness, patience, renunciation, wisdom, determination, honesty, diligence, and equanimity. These are essential qualities for living in happiness and peace.

I feel the cultivation of the Ten Perfections is sorely lacking in the practice of many meditators, and this prevents them from truly reaping the fruits of this wonderful path. Students who engage in my online course of the Ten Perfections invariably experience massive transformations in their lives, and along this path. The intention to cultivate these *pāramī* sets in motion Right Effort, and I would strongly encourage you to explore each of them in every aspect of your life.

I discuss more elements of Right Effort in the next chapter ('The Devil is in the Details'), and ways of abandoning and preventing detrimental qualities you possess in the following one, 'The Singular Cause of Your Suffering.'

Right Intention in Buddhism includes all dependent arisings (*paticcasamuppada*) and not simply some singular intent. My intention to write this included sitting down, composing my thoughts, and pressing the keys, etc. Intentions compete and overlap with each other, or one may replace another, if our motivations are not entirely aligned.

Gradually, we grow our awareness of this interrelated co-dependency rather than focusing on basic cause to effect. Right Intention also includes things we choose and choose not to do. This leads to deeper understanding and the ability to avoid unskilful thoughts and actions.

As I have tried to show, each of these spokes is intricately related to the others. The more you are able to *stabilise your attention*, *prioritise your actions*, *open your awareness*, and *kindle your understanding*, the more you can *expand your world*. This enables you to direct your intention and effort towards your chosen goal(s). In other words, when your aspirations (spokes) are aligned, every action you take is one step closer to living more freely with less stress, and ultimately to living free from suffering.

CHAPTER 3
THE DEVIL IS IN THE DETAILS

This chapter deals with the 'U' part of the missing ingredients to awakening: urgency and unflappability. Spiritual urgency feels like a call from deep within that does not subside; like a strong pull into an abyss. It can feel simultaneously terrifying as it feels exciting. Either way, you are drawn towards an unknown, and the best things to do when this happens is to explore every nuance of your experience in life, on and off the cushion.

Some people have used various psychoactive substances to explore their spirituality. I have, in the past, worked with a number of people after they have had eye-opening, but confusing and sometimes terrifying, psychedelic trips. Similarly, I have worked with people who have spontaneously awakened in their teens or early twenties, and then found me decades later after wondering if they, or the world, had gone mad. I have also worked with people who, like me, spontaneously found themselves lost in the Dark Night period after intense meditation practice. These people have all always been palpably relieved when I put their experiences within a framework of this path and shined a light for them as I walked alongside them towards a more open space of safety, understanding, and freedom.

Perhaps you are among those who fear the possibility of the destabilising effects of this path, and this prevents you from exploring further. I would like to assure you that such rough landings are not the norm, and with the right practices, they do not have to occur at all. Awakening to the reality of our existence is a wondrous thing, and integrating this understanding into the fabric of all of existence is a fascinating, ongoing exploration. The trick is to balance urgency with unflappability, constant investigation with equanimity.

Equanimity (*upekkhā*) is one of the seven factors of awakening. This is a state of even temperament where the experiences of life are met by a mind in a state of perfect equilibrium. Equanimity protects you from the destabilising effects mentioned before. When present, the waves of life are perceived as not as large and are met with equipoise.

Many people with a natural aptitude for concentration gravitate towards *samatha* practices to further stabilise their attention into meditation states known as the *jhānas*. Equanimity borne of this sort of one-pointedness is often mistaken for the end of the path. It is not.

You can get very skilled at just relaxing and calming the mind, such that *dukkha* is no longer seen even when it is there. In other words, this sort of one-pointed equanimity can simply temporarily suppress the experience of *dukkha* while awareness has collapsed.

Some students are interested in exploring the *jhānas* practices. When I teach *jhānas*, I tell my more experienced students that whilst mastery of the *jhānas* is useful, more important is their practice after exiting the *jhāna*. You should consider the time at which you exit a *jhāna* (particularly the 4th *jhāna*, when there is a lot of focus and equanimity) as the half-way point of that particular meditation sit. Using your mind that is now sharp from one-pointedness, you should re-engage your awareness and start your practice of *vipassanā* to explore the intrinsic nature of the mind and discover what would not have been apparent to a less-pliant and less-sharp mind. By opening your awareness and incorporating the awakening factor of investigation (*dhamma vicaya*) at this juncture, the nature of the three characteristics of impermanence (*aniccā*), non-self (*anattā*) and unsatisfactoriness or suffering (*dukkha*) can be illuminated with lucidity, thereby allowing insights to arise.

True equanimity is borne of the wisdom of these insights into *aniccā*, *dukkha* and *anattā*. Despite the inevitable vicissitudes of life, insights into *dukkha* and its causes and conditions give rise to the wisdom to ride the waves of our experiences. Irrespective of circumstances, all of life can now be truly experienced from an equidistant vantage and maintained with equipoise.

Students who do not heed my advice and instead continue to exclusively practise the *jhānas* have a tendency to continue to suppress their *dukkha*. They can become irritated or annoyed without being aware of this. They remain unaware of the myriad feelings they may be experiencing, unconsciously clinging to the belief that they are still equanimous. I have seen this far too often, and feel it is a shame that such dedicated practitioners get stuck in this unconscious clinging.

A quick review of the difference between attention and awareness, the two different ways our brains allow us to perceive the world, may help elucidate this. *Samatha* practices train in the stability of attention. By nature, attention perceives things as discrete and detailed. The training of one-pointedness that leads to the *jhānas* is the epitome of the training in attention. This results in an incredible amount of peace and calm. The narrow focus into one-pointed attention, however, also comes at a cost of temporarily losing perspective of what else is present.

Awareness, unlike attention, is more panoramic in nature. If it collapses, all you are left with is the experiences of your narrow attention. After a *jhāna*, your mind is calm and pliant. If you open your awareness at this juncture to include the entirety of your other experiences and begin the practice of *vipassanā*, you can use this broader perspective to discover aspects of your existence from a different vantage. This results in a clearer comprehension of the wisdom of the *Dhamma*.

To mistake equanimity with awakening is to miss the treasure of the *Dhamma*. *Samatha* and *vipassanā* are said to be like the two wings of a bird, allowing it to soar with peace and wisdom. Although awareness is involved, *samatha* is largely the training of attention, resulting in equanimity and stability. *Vipassanā* uses the faculty of strong awareness to explore the gestalt of our experiences and their interrelationships, resulting in the emergence of insight and wisdom. Ultimately training in the optimal balance between stable attention and powerful awareness, the two different ways in which we attend to the world, is what brings both peace and wisdom into your life.

Because I no longer teach in retreat settings, preferring to help people apply this practice in their everyday lives (which I personally see as a major need among our community of meditators), I encourage people who are interested in mastering the *jhānas* to attend retreats with the handful of experts on these practices, who are far more qualified than I am to teach this very refined art. The important thing I highlight remains, though: utilise your sharp mind in service of understanding the true nature of our existence; do not waste your *jhāna* experiences by lingering *ad infinitum* in these states.

I named this chapter 'The Devil Is in the Details' because I truly believe that the only way to fully awaken is to explore, in every moment of your waking life, every nuance of what the Buddha taught. Explore the ten *pāramī*, one at a time, and several in conjunction with each other. Investigate the three characteristics, the presence of the *jhāna* factors, and the seven factors of awakening (*bojjhaṅgā*). Explore these individually, and the balance of each awakening factor with relation to the others. Recognise when they are present and when they are not. Explore what causes and conditions seem to precede their emergence, and which ones seem to precede their lack of arising.

Do all of this very regularly throughout your day. Your experiences in life are wonderful fodder for awakening to the reality of your existence. I have personally met many more people who have had profound insights into the *Dhamma* occur in their daily lives rather than in seated meditations. While it is true that you can explore very subtle nuances of the path during seated meditations, it is also true that constant exploration of the practice off the cushion increases the probability of you understanding the true nature of reality. And the reality is, even during retreats, the most one spends in seated meditation is around eight hours a day. There are still another eight to ten waking hours to engage in this practice!

As I write this, I realise that this can sound like a very intense and tedious practice. It is not. It is, in fact, quite the opposite. It is a very gentle exploration that you engage in because you are truly curious. If you tell children there is a treasure hunt, they may spend hours upon hours engaged in the exploration, excited and energetic. When we adopt this same attitude of playful curiosity, this becomes very conducive to opening into the fundamental nature and possibilities of our existence.

The question, 'What is happening in this moment?' is all you need to kick-start the process. If your connection with your awareness has been 'off-line' for a little while, the question can help you to immediately recognise that you are sitting, standing, walking, or lying down, that you are breathing, that the temperature is warm or cold. Upon asking yourself this question, you may instead tune in to your faculty of hearing and suddenly be aware *of* the sounds around you, or realise *that* you are actually hearing. Do you understand the difference here? You may be aware of the sounds, and *that* you are hearing—two different points of awareness. The same goes for seeing: You can notice *what* you are seeing, and *that* you are seeing.

As you continue connecting to an awareness that is receptive to all of your experiences, this becomes a habitual way in which you interact with the world more astutely and more consciously. This invariably leads to an ability to notice more subtle nuances of what is present in each moment. You may start becoming more aware of the subtleties of what is known as your *metacognitive introspective state of being*. Whereas you could initially always know that you were stressed, and the level of stress you were experiencing, this stronger awareness would open to the precursors of this, such as the emergence of mild irritation, annoyance, or agitation. You become more sensitive to any changes experienced, which gives you more precise control over what you can do, and when.

Choice is not the only thing available to you with

stronger awareness. Because your mind now has access to a vast array of information coming from all your senses (including metacognitively), you become accustomed to seeing the complexities of life and stop the simple cause-and-effect assumptions to which we so often succumb. For example, a student of mine believed that she was constantly anxious because of a particular incident with her brother that she had labelled as bullying. She had metaphorically been pointing her finger directly at him, blaming him for the difficulties in her life that resulted from his one action.

As her awareness increased through this practice, without trying to think of this time of her life at all, a host of different memories suddenly appeared to her as she was watching her children argue one day. She remembered taunting her brother incessantly and the moment he 'snapped.' She recalled his remorse thereafter and her refusal to accept his apology. She recalled a sudden decision as a child that she was not going to forgive him—ever.

There were other memories of her childhood that she suddenly had access to as well. She recalled that prior to the incident, she tended to be more twitchy than other people. She recalled how she taunted people around her when she felt anxious, almost as a way to take control in the midst of an otherwise uncontrollable nervous system. Even as a child prior to this incident with her brother, she hated the feeling of anxiety, and seemed to unconsciously take it out on others or shut down into herself when these feelings arose. She reflected on her continued tendency to do this now, which inadvertently led to long bouts of consuming social media, binge eating or outbursts at people around her, and the subsequent shame and guilt of losing control of herself.

I explained that it was wonderful that she had realised all this. The fact that she could describe these patterns of her mind meant that her awareness was good. And did she remember what the practice was when she recognised that she was present? Smile and appreciate that her awareness is doing its job! Just like the preliminary practice of appreciating awareness increased its frequency and potency, continuing to use positive reinforcement to cultivate this subtler form of awareness was the best thing to do.

With patience and repetition, she learnt to shift from the shame and guilt of remembering her past actions, and getting stuck in those memories, to recognising that she was *aware* of her shame and guilt. At this meta level of awareness, she was momentarily free from shame and guilt and able to choose to appreciate the awareness instead. This reinforced the awareness and allowed her to regain control of her mind, away from being trapped by the vortex of the shame and guilt.

With greater awareness and constant exploration of every single phenomenon we encounter in life, and in conjunction with strong equanimity, we start seeing the very interconnectedness of all of our existence. Instead of seeing ourselves as individual nodes in a system, we realise that we are the actual network; we are, in reality, the inextricably linked connections.

I encourage my students to use silent meditation retreat time to explore this in detail, as well as build their stability of attention. I also emphasise that they use the rest of their daily lives to continue what they have established during retreats, in order to really experience the profundity of these teachings.

One of my students recently did exactly this. She built a strong stability of mind during retreat and continued exploring the nature of reality when driving home. As she was driving, she suddenly had a transformative insight into the reality of our existence.

The vast majority of people I know who have had transformative insights have experienced this while continuing the exploration off the cushion. Please don't think that meditation in the seated posture, or meditation retreats, are the only times you can awaken. This is a practice of real life; apply it to everything in life and you will see for yourself.

I'd like to conclude this chapter with my perspective on what I see as 'the equanimity confusion.' As readers of this part of the book probably know, *upekkhā* (equanimity) is one of the four *brahmavihārās*, or Divine Abidings, also known as the Four Immeasurables. The other three are *mettā* (loving-kindness), *karuṇā* (compassion), and *muditā* (empathetic joy).

Because of our tendency to put things into hierarchies, meditators often put equanimity at the top of the hierarchy. It is important to refrain from doing this. These four Divine Abidings are states that naturally arise from different circumstances. Being equanimous does not mean you do not feel emotions; it means there is always a sense of okayness, irrespective of what you feel.

For example, one of my students had been mastering the *jhānas* on retreat. As a consequence, her mind was sublimely refined and equanimous. Nothing could touch her peace of mind. At home the night after her retreat ended, she received a phone call from a hospital, telling her that her daughter had been in a car accident and had been taken there. Unfortunately, she did not hear which hospital her daughter was in.

Over the next two hours, she systematically (not frantically) called all the hospitals in the region where the accident occurred. Eventually, she managed to find where her daughter was. Composed and clear thinking, she got herself to the hospital, where she found her daughter with multiple fractures across her head and body.

My student spent the whole evening sitting calmly by her daughter's side, hoping that the same peace of mind she felt would be shared with her daughter. Her daughter did not make it through the night. My student knew that her daughter had died peacefully and was grateful that she was able to be there with her until the very end.

She spoke to me with tears streaming down her face. Her equanimity meant that she was at peace with her heart being torn open with grief. She was also able to feel grateful for the kind support of everyone around her, be filled with compassion towards her own mother who had collapsed with distraught in her arms, and smile with joy at the memory of her daughter's remarkable life that had been cut short. She inhabited the entirety of the Divine Abidings in the most appropriate human ways.

CHAPTER 4
THE SINGULAR CAUSE OF YOUR SUFFERING

This chapter refines the compass you hold to ensure the course correction you take in every moment of your day is directly in line with the *Dhamma*. This is the practice of the Second Noble Truth, the truth of the cause of suffering.

Taṇhā, translated as thirst, craving, desire, or longing, is this cause of our suffering. *Taṇhā* is the difference between what is happening in this moment and what you would *like* to be happening. The larger this difference, the stronger your suffering.

Taṇhā can manifest in two different ways: *dosa* (aversion, non-wanting, wanting to escape an experience) and *lobha* (greed, wanting something, wanting more). These two types of *taṇhā* are based on *moha* (delusion). Rather than theoretically go through these three 'poisons' or unwholesome roots, it is more useful to understand the experience of each of these as they arise. A good way to do this is to explore the physical correlates of these mind states.

Every mind state we have has a physical correlation. What I mean by this is that there is always some 'tell' of the body that indicates what we are experiencing in our mind. Otherwise, we would not be able to experience it. For example, when a student tells me they are feeling angry, I often ask, 'How do you know you are angry?' Of course, I am met with a perplexed look, to which I say, 'What changes have happened in your body to indicate to you that you are angry?'

This question turns your attention away from the *cause* of your anger, towards your *experience* of anger. Moreover, it is the physical experience of your anger towards which I am deliberately encouraging you to direct your attention. What do you notice when you are angry? Just think about the various similes and metaphors that relate to anger: 'fuming with anger,' 'seeing red,' 'as angry as a charging bull,' 'blind' with anger, 'boiling blood,' 'hot under the collar,' 'exploding/erupting with anger,' 'have steam coming out of your ears,' and so forth.

These give signs of what we universally experience in anger—an excess of heat and energy. When you are angry, you might feel a lot of heat in certain parts of your body. Which parts? How far does this extend? Does it remain stagnant or change in gross or subtle ways with time? All these are useful questions to ask yourself to increase your awareness of this phenomenon of anger.

Alternatively, you may feel an excess of energy coursing through your body and feel you need to 'blow off steam.' As always, when you are aware of or conscious about your experiences, you have a choice of what you do at this point. If you are not sufficiently aware, you will likely fall into the habitual, unconscious patterns of continuing to look towards the perceived cause of your anger ('it was because that person cut me off in traffic' or 'that person defamed me by saying …'). You may then react in your normal way of ranting and raging about the incident to people around you, or replaying it in your mind. All this does is to re-expose your brain to the trigger, thereby increasing your anger.

If instead you see that your anger is not serving you well and is causing you more suffering, you are then in a position to do something about it. The moment you are aware, it is possible to choose to appreciate the reprieve provided by the awareness; and then, in order to take the anger down a notch, consciously redirect your attention to something else, such as taking a few deep breaths, or noticing something else that is present that will not exacerbate your anger. These are the foundational practices we developed in Part Two.

If you have cultivated sufficient equanimity in your practice, another way of exploring anger is now open to you. As mentioned above, instead of looking at the *trigger* of your anger, you can explore the *experience* of anger. As discussed, you can explore *how* anger feels in your body. You may *think* you know, but how does it *actually* feel in this moment of time? Can you notice the changes involved in this one, solid word of 'anger'?

Every concept is, by definition, rigid. When we have concepts or ideas in our minds, we affix permanency to them. They become real and immutable. The word 'anger' is very solid. When anger is present, it is not possible to simultaneously feel love. The experience of one precludes the other.

While words and concepts tend to have an immutably quality to them, experiences are in constant flux. Directing your attention onto your bodily sensations that seem to be associated with anger may start with you noticing a lot of energy in your body. You may notice movement in your stomach as if you were about to run a race. You may notice tightness in your chest as well as burning heat in your face. If you stay with noticing your bodily sensations, you may become aware of the fact that the tightness has now moved to feel like a clenched fist in your stomach, and the 'butter-flies in the stomach' are no longer there. You may also notice that your face has the characteristic feeling of redness (even without looking in a mirror).

Being aware of your experiences over a period of time allows you to see the ever-changing nature of the flux of life. Rather than reify your experiences, are you able to open to other possibilities of what this experience can teach you? Start truly exploring the experience of anger, rather than continue in the endless cycle of justifying it.

The next stage of this practice is to start noticing more subtle reactions of the mind when you experience anger. Whenever there is an unpleasant sensation, can you discern the sense of 'This is happening. I don't want this to happen! I hate this!'? This is a more refined practice that can only occur once your awareness is strong enough. The prerequisites to this practice are:

1. Strong enough awareness, built through positive reinforcement that leads to an automatic appreciation of awareness whenever it is present (Part Two practices).
2. Acknowledgement that anger is causing more harm than good to you (recognising there is *dukkha*).
3. Ability to explore bodily sensations related to anger from a space of equanimity and curiosity (part of what is known as *kāyānupassanā*).
4. Ability to discern and explore the pleasant, unpleasant, and more neutral aspects of each

sensation, from a space of equanimity and
curiosity (what is known as *vedanānupassanā*).

Only when you have stabilised your practice in the
above are you ready to embark on looking at what is known
as *cittanupassanā*, mindfulness of the mind. In this case, we
are exploring the existence of *dosa*, often translated as 'aversion' or 'ill-will.'

What are the bodily correlates of aversion? How does
this mind state manifest in the body? Can you discern its
characteristics? The exploration of aversion needs to start
with these questions that are invitations to explore this with
curiosity. They are not intended to be answered conceptually, but rather experientially.

I find that this exploration requires a lot more of a
hands-on approach in coaching students on the subtleties of
this practice. However, for the sake of completion, I will
describe what I often say to students after they have
engaged in the exploration of *dosa* to a deeper extent. At this
point, I encourage students to notice the antecedents and
consequences of the *dosa* that has arisen. To what extent are
you able to trace the causes and conditions of the *dosa*, as
well as recognise the extent of the consequences? How
much of a bigger perspective of the network of interconnectedness on this are you able to see? How much of the process
are you able to ascertain through your investigation of this
mind state of *dosa*?

These are all simply pointers. Even if I could describe
what I experience when engaging in this exploration, it
would not be of any benefit to you, because it is not your
own experience. Patiently and slowly start engaging in this
practice, starting from Part Two, and only later build upon
the foundations. Even if you have been practising for a long

time and think you know about this, always start with a beginner's mind, in order to discover more of what lies in our remarkable world.

Lobha, often translated as 'greed,' has a different flavour. It feels like a lurching towards an object or experience that is not present. Do you remember that I defined *taṇhā* as the difference between what is happening in this moment and what you would like to be happening? In *lobha*, you don't perceive what is happening right now as sufficient. You want more. You want that *jhāna* experience. Or you want to have more wisdom or equanimity. Or you want so much to awaken.

But you want this in a way that is causing you suffering. Rather than holding these noble goals as aspirations, you cling to the idea of these with greed. And in so doing, you create more *dukkha* for yourself, which is the exact opposite direction to where you wish to head.

Think of a goal not as something to strive forcefully towards, but as a direction to point your compass. You are sailing your ship and the only thing you need to do is course correct and gently direct the bow towards your destination. Your job is not to frantically try to power the vessel by jumping off the ship and trying to push it by swimming behind it. It is simply to keep your eye on the destination and regularly steer to stay on course.

Noticing *taṇhā* allows you to immediately know that your ship has drifted off course. I often say to my students that anytime you are suffering, it is an alarm bell to remind you that you have drifted off course. Understanding the nature of *taṇhā* allows you to predict times it is likely to arise, as well as more effectively course correct when it is present. This practice happens both on and off the cushion. In your daily life, you have many opportunities to observe the arising of *taṇhā*, and the better you have cultivated your ability to be aware of it, the more you can explore the process.

The third unwholesome root is *moha*, often translated as delusion or confusion. The experiential aspect of this is very subtle and difficult to describe. I first clearly saw the arising of *moha* during my very first meditation retreat with Sayadaw U Tejaniya. I had been exploring *lobha*, that subtle lurching forward towards everything I anticipated—that next mouthful of food as it approached, or that next step towards the bed at the end of the day. I had also been exploring *dosa*, that subtle resistance to anything whatsoever that was unpleasant—the bright sun, the sudden loud noise, the surge of anxiety.

Watching the clear arising of *dosa* and *lobha* was the most interesting thing I had come across in a long time. Who would have thought I would find greed and aversion more fascinating and enticing to explore than peace and serenity? I realised I had found the missing piece to my practice.

As I explored the seemingly opposing reactions of lurching away from my present experience (*dosa*) and lurching towards a different experience (*lobha*), I suddenly saw that they were two sides of the same coin, with delusion (*moha*) the actual coin. *Moha* has a confused state associated with it, like a spinning coin uncertain of whether it is going to land on *dosa* or *lobha*. Like a dog chasing its tail, *moha* has the characteristic feel of fogginess, confusion, spinning, and uncertainty. Needless to say, once I could discern and explore the extremely subtle mind state of *moha*, as well as the arising of non-greed (i.e., generosity), non-aversion (i.e., loving-kindness) and non-delusion (i.e., wisdom), things moved to an entirely different dimension.

Life with *taṇhā* is like having a constant itch that needs to be scratched. We confuse the process of alleviating the itch with contentment. Through *lobha*, we want something we do not have, get it, and are temporarily satisfied. Our minds then move to wishing to experience something else, work towards it, and then again are temporarily satisfied if we achieve it, and filled with *dosa* if we do not. And so the cycle continues.

Taṇhā is the invisible driving force that propels you in all sorts of directions, unconsciously and aimlessly. Temporary relief is the very opposite of contentment. When you patiently work towards understanding *taṇhā*, it will naturally uproot itself and you will never have to be at the mercy of that itch again.

CHAPTER 5
FREEING THE MIND

The final pair of missing ingredients to awakening relates to enjoyment and environment. Each time you recognise that awareness is present and smile in appreciation of it, you are encouraging its future emergence through positive reinforcement. You are doing this by connecting with the simplicity and beauty of being conscious, and appreciating it. This appreciation then extends to the cultivation of joy, one of the seven factors of awakening, and culminates in the savouring of all aspects of our exquisite existence.

Environment relates to *sangha,* a like-minded community of people who support and encourage each other. Belonging to such a group increases enjoyment and provides inspiration and support along this path.

I teach mainly in groups. The most common response I hear from meditators when they first consider working with me is that they don't like group activities because they are introverts. I have to remind them that the majority of us meditators are introverts! We choose, after all, to spend our time meditating in silence and solitude, cultivating our introspection!

This does not preclude us from belonging to a *saṅgha*, a community of like-minded people. Nothing replaces human connection. Support of a *saṅgha* is essential in this process. When treading this path, you can easily veer off course. A suitable mentor is essential in order to make effective progress and a *saṅgha* will make this journey more efficient and enjoyable.

Contrary to popular imagery, this is not a path we engage in alone. Through the solitude of our meditative explorations, we learn about our collectiveness. Through independence, we learn about our interconnectedness. Don't conflate individual aspects of the practice for the path. Any form of dichotomising, of creating a sense of separation, is not the *Dhamma*. We are not the nodes of the network; we are the connections. Embrace connection through belonging to a *saṅgha.*

Enjoyment itself is just as important as connecting with like-minded people. Some students have difficulty with the cultivation of *pīti*, or joy. This usually relates to some rigid concept they have formed around the term. They hear or read about the five kinds of *pīti* that can arise through the practice of tranquillity and usually fixate on one or two of these. Thereafter, they don't consider any of their experiences as sufficiently matching this concept of *pīti* and miss the whole point of the cultivation of joy.

I usually encourage students to start by being on the lookout for any pleasant feeling or sensation (*vedanā*). When this happens, enjoy it. Spend a few moments savouring the pleasantness of the feeling. Instead of being fixated on some concept of 'joy,' enjoy the pleasant sensations when they are present.

Enjoying pleasant sensations when they arise helps create the positive feedback loops in the brain that encourage awareness in general, and awareness of pleasant sensations specifically. The mind is now better tuned to the arising of this *vedanā* and ready for the more refined practice of *vedanānupassana*, the mindfulness of feeling tones. Cultivate this first before going on to *cittānupassana*, mindfulness of the mind.

Can you notice the presence of pleasant *vedanā*? Can you enjoy its pleasantness? Can you clearly discern the difference between pleasant *vedanā* and *lobha* (greed)? Does *lobha* arise at times, and not at other times? What are the possible causes and conditions, as well as the possible consequences of the presence, or absence, of *lobha*? Can you see the network of interconnections of the entirety of the system that relates to the starting point of pleasant *vedanā*? These are some of the more refined practices to which clear-seeing of pleasant sensations can lead.

This practice relies entirely on the ongoing cultivation of awareness, and enjoyment is an essential factor in this process. Through powerful awareness, we can free our mind from the illusion of separateness and see the interconnected wholeness of our existence. When we are not riddled with our various reactions to our experiences, we can open ourselves to savour the entirety of our wondrous existence.

I am often asked what the experience of freedom from *dukkha* feels like. Perhaps my current experience can serve as an example. I am currently recovering from an illness. I feel like there is an elephant sitting on my chest. Its trunk is wrapped around my head, squeezing it around the temples in a most uncomfortable way. But I am calm, equanimous, and content. I am sitting here in the midst of the physical discomfort, enjoying the process of connecting with you through my writing.

Through trusting the wisdom that arises from awareness, I am conscious of when I need to rest the body and when I need to take a break. I trust the process entirely, never needing to second-guess myself. I think this is the most significant aspect of understanding this path. People are often surprised at how much I get done in a day. I feel this is directly related to the fact that rather than fighting life, I trust the process entirely, and live life riding the currents of the stream.

I see many students waste precious time and energy by accusing others, second-guessing themselves, and doubting the process. Instead of learning to flow with life, they seem to regularly get stuck in its eddies. The experience of awakening is freeing. It doesn't mean that life no longer presents challenges, but rather that there is no resistance to them whatsoever. All that is left is interest and curiosity about what is happening in each moment. As I said to someone yesterday, what goes through my mind with regards to this elephant on my chest is the question, 'I wonder if this elephant is going to move?' rather than 'I wish this elephant would go away!' The difference is a segue from the hubris of the reality-resisting self to the humility and acceptance of our place within this beautifully vast network.

The thing I most often say to my more advanced students is, 'Trust the process. You have done the work already; you can let go now and enjoy the flow of the *Dhamma*.' When they do this, they invariably progress further along the stream.

What of life afterwards? As the Zen saying goes, 'Before enlightenment: chop wood, carry water. After enlightenment: chop wood, carry water.' Life continues as it does, but you no longer quarrel with it. You smile, learn, explore, and connect more and more deeply with every facet, every person, and every nuance of life.

Sometimes, people feel they need to give up their jobs, their families, their hobbies, and their friends in their pursuit of spiritual awakening. It may well be the case that at some point along the journey, you feel compelled to do this. On the other hand, it may be the case that you do not have the option to renounce the world. The intention of this book is to inspire you to realise that you do not have to give up everything to follow this path. This path is about letting go of suffering; it is not about letting go of life.

To the contrary, fully walking the path means fully embracing all of life. I recently met up with an old friend who told me that her son had taken his own life. My heart opened fully to my friend and her family, as tears flowed freely from both our eyes. Life is poignant. To what extent can you fully embrace the entirety of all of life? Deeply connecting with the pain and sorrow of someone else's grief can be as liberating as deeply connecting with the exquisite joys of life. In the appreciation of the fleeting nature of life, one fully experiences the preciousness of all of existence without resistance.

Equanimity is not about being unfeeling. Equanimity is being totally okay with fully feeling the impact and significance of life because of, not despite, the enormity of it all. It is not about keeping a distance from life. The four *brahmavihārās* of equanimity, compassion, loving-kindness, and empathetic joy are actually rolled in one natural, appropriate response to life's ebbs and flows.

Living without the aversion of constantly trying to push unpleasant experiences away, without the greed of constantly trying to maintain current pleasant experiences or moving towards more pleasant experiences, or the delusion of not knowing when you are spinning rapidly between greed and aversion, results in a certain lightness of being. There is no clinging to the weight of life, through repulsion or attraction. All of the experiences of life are welcomed, embraced, and let go of, like the serendipitous meeting of good friends in a busy airport.

Sometimes, one is inextricably called to engage in an onerous and seemingly impossible task. With the lightness of being that comes with the liberation of the mind, one goes along with things, trusting the process and seeing what happens. This is my experience with the platform I have set up. You see, I contracted a viral encephalitis four years ago which resulted in somewhat serious consequences. In addition to experiencing severe, chronic headaches, I was left with severe issues with my working memory, which resulted in confusion.

At the time, I lost my ability to read and follow the simplest of sentences. I would technically be able to read a sentence like 'the cat sat on the mat,' but was unable to understand the meaning of the sentence. I understood only the puzzling image of a bulge under a mat and was confused as to what I was supposed to do with that image. Someone would say a sentence to me, and I would understand individual words but not be able to follow what the sentences meant. I remember saying that I felt that my IQ had dropped 30 points as I just couldn't understand what people around me were saying.

I had to stop working as a psychotherapist and could no longer teach meditation. I could barely move from one room to another without being totally confused about why I was there and what I was supposed to do. Doctors' appointments were a matter of waiting for months, and endless scans and tests that resulted in no plan of action that could be taken.

With the help of friends, I eventually came up with a single list of action steps for the rehabilitation of my brain. This was basically a list for the prevention, or slowing, of dementia. At the time, we had no idea if there was ever going to be any improvement in my condition whatsoever, so I focused on trying to ensure it did not get even worse. I started drinking green tea, intermittently fasting, learning a new language, juggling, doing inane brain exercises on my computer, learning a new instrument, and exercising outdoors daily. My husband stopped work and I spent my time engaging in these activities as we travelled and lived in a truck in the outback of Australia.

The salient aspect of this period is the attitude of mind that was always prevalent within me. I was always happy, content, and willing to embrace each new experience with openness, interest, and acceptance. I did not once resist any of my experiences. I was, and remain, like a happy goldfish: always ready to savour and embrace each and every moment of life.

I think the most challenging aspect of my disability was with relation to others. I was, at times, incapable of communicating effectively, as words either failed me, or a cacophony of multiple languages I had learnt in the past came out of my mouth as I tried to express myself. At other times, I was seemingly 'normal,' and my husband and children had to somehow remember that the fiercely independent and capable person they knew still had significantly reduced capacities.

On my more lucid days, they often did not remember, and I would have to sometimes quite forcefully remind them that my brain was really not capable of executing certain functions, and that although I was sometimes able to find workarounds that covered this fact, I did truly need help for some things. The basic tenets of Right Speech had to always prevail: truthful, beneficial, timely, pleasant, and imbued with loving-kindness.

I keep the compass of Right Speech always in mind, and remember that whenever I need to communicate something, it is because the other party does not yet know it. The onus is on me to somehow find a way to get the message across, and my experience is that it is only through more deeply connecting with awareness and my deepest aspirations that I am able to somehow succeed, often through a combination of words, gestures, and examples.

How can I convey my essential needs in a way that is imbued with loving-kindness, for myself as well as for others? Holding the line of compassion for myself by clearly, yet kindly, expressing my needs in a way that can be heard by others is part of my dance of life.

Wisdom that arises from awareness allows for creative solutions. Rather than being restricted by the conceptual framework of our habitual patterns of mind, we are let into the vastness of possibilities. We inhabit not just the sometimes faulty node, but the entirety of the wondrous network of connections.

Because in the first two years of my illness I managed to rehabilitate my brain to a certain extent, and because of the platform I managed to set up in the subsequent year, people assume that my brain is normal again (Or even worse, they sometimes assume I am some sort of a genius who can easily get things done without effort). It is not, and I am not. I ask others for help. I pay people to help me do things I am unable to do. I rely on the kindness of loved ones and strangers alike. I live the connections.

My life's compass points to helping more people to awaken to the reality of the end of *dukkha*. It is a strange compass that I have inexplicably found myself holding; it feels like this is beyond a calling for me, and I humbly accept the challenge. Despite my natural discomfort of revealing so much of my personal life in a public forum, I have laid myself bare in a sincere effort to inspire others to know that this path is possible, and possible for everyone who wishes to walk it, irrespective of their life's circumstances.

EPILOGUE: YOUR TURN

When I meet someone, I often wish they could see themselves the way I see them. Their wonderful characteristics of kindness, sincerity, and dedication shine brightly to my eyes. But all too often, when they see themselves, they only see the parts of themselves that need improving, overlooking the vast majority of their positive attributes.

While it may be true that there are always things to be improved, if your attention is focused too much on this, you miss the forest for the trees. Instead of seeing yourself as the separate and faulty node in a vast network that needs to compete with other nodes in order to survive, learning to befriend yourself opens you to the bigger reality of inhabiting the network of interconnections that we really are.

Try this out for yourself. Acknowledge your stress when it is present and seek the wisdom to untangle yourself from the web of it. Align your values and build your awareness. Appreciate the precious and fleeting nature of our existence on earth in order to understand the importance of learning the skills of unflappability in the face of urgency. Incline your mind towards contentment and wisdom, and use this as your compass for regular course correction. And finally, remember that enjoyability and environment are essential on this path. Find a community of learners, good mentors and teachers, and merge with the beauty of our precious, poignant existence.

You've got this. Or what I really mean is, we've got this!

GLOSSARY

This glossary represents the way I have used these terms in this book.

Ahimsa: non-harming; gentleness to all forms of life

Anattā: non-self; non-ego identification

Aniccā: impermanence or flux of life

Asaṅga's *Elephant Path*: 9 stage path to Calm-Abiding by Asaṅga, one of the most important spiritual figures in Mahāyāna Buddhism

Aversion: the mental pushing away of an unpleasant experience

Bojjhaṅgās: 7 factors to be cultivated for enlightenment or awakening

Brahmavihārās: 4 virtues of loving-kindness, compassion, empathetic joy and equanimity

Cittānupassanā: observation or exploration of the mind

Dark Night of the Soul: known as *dukkha-ñāṇas, part of the path to purification experienced* by some spiritual seekers

Dhamma: the laws of our universe, as expressed by the teachings of the Buddha

Dhamma vicaya: investigation or discernment of the *Dhamma*

Dhammacakka: *widespread symbol of the wheel of the Dhamma*

Dosa: see aversion

Dukkha: fundamental unsatisfactoriness and stress this practice aims to transcend

Ehipassiko: A teaching by the Buddha to not accept things based on what you hear, but rather 'come and see for yourself'

Four Immeasurables: see *Brahmavihārās*

Jhānas: deep meditative absorptions

Karuṇā: compassion (towards oneself and others)

Kāyānupassanā: observation or exploration of the body

Lobha: greed, or the mental moving towards a pleasant experience

Mahāmudrā: an advanced Tibetan Buddhist meditation practice

Mahāsī method: Meditation practice introduced by Burmese monk Mahāsi Sayādaw

Metacognitive introspection: observation and exploration of the activities of the mind

Mettā: loving-kindness, goodwill and friendliness (towards oneself and others)

Micchā diṭṭhi: wrong or distorted view

Moha: fundamental delusion inherent in all people who are not fully enlightened

Muditā: empathetic joy or the joy one feels in the good fortune of others

Noble Eightfold Path: the eight practices for the attainment of *nibbāna*

Paccavekkhana-ñāna: stage of insight that follows Path and Fruition Knowledges of nibbāna

Pāramī: ten perfections or fundamental human qualities

associated with enlightened beings. These are generosity, virtue, renunciation, wisdom, diligence, patience, truthfulness, determination, loving-kindness and equanimity.

Paṭiccasamuppāda: profound Buddhist understanding of the dependent arising of all phenomena

Pīti: experience of the energising quality of joy

Samatha: meditation practice that trains the mind in stability of attention that leads to peace, calm and stillness

Samatha-vipassanā: yoked meditation practice that simultaneously trains the mind in stability of attention and cultivation of vivid awareness for the attainment of *nibbāna*

Sammā-ājīva: the practice of wise livelihood, as described in the Noble Eightfold Path

Sammā-diṭṭhi: wise view, or wise knowledge of the Four Noble Truths

Sammā-kammanta: the practice of wise action, as described in the Noble Eightfold Path

Sammā-samādhi: the practice of wise concentration; the picking of a suitable meditation object for the current circumstances constitutes an important part of this

Sammā-saṅkappa: wise intention. Intention governs every action and inaction we take, and has profound consequences. Being more conscious or aware of our intentions allows us to cultivate wise intention, as described in the Noble Eightfold Path

Sammā-sati: wise mindfulness or awareness is crucial on this path to liberation

Sammā-vācā: wise speech, speech that is truthful, beneficial, timely and imbued with lovingkindness

Sammā-vāyāma: wise effort aims to cultivate beneficial qualities of the mind and reduce or eliminate detrimental qualities that cause harm to oneself and others

Saṅgha: a community of like-minded practitioners dedicated to the Buddhist path

Second Noble Truth: Part of the Four Noble Truths related to the cause of suffering

Sutta: Buddhist scripture

Taṇhā: thirst or craving for things to be other than they are. The cause of our suffering

Upekkhā: equanimity, the quality of even-temperament

Vedanā: feeling tone, valence or hedonic tone of experiences

Vedanānupassanā: mindfulness or exploration of feeling tones

Vipassanā: a special way of clear seeing that leads to wisdom related to awareness

Visuddhimagga: 5th century systematisation of the Buddhist path to enlightenment

Zen beginner's mind: an attitude of openness, interest and lack of preconceptions

ABOUT THE AUTHOR

Li-Anne Tang is a Buddhist meditation teacher who is committed to helping people free themselves from stress and suffering.

She is married and has two adult children. Her academic background includes a Bachelor of Psychology, a Master of Cognitive Science, a Ph.D. in neuropsychiatry and postgraduate training in psychoanalytic psychotherapy.

Since 2008 she has closely mentored her students in the styles of Sayadaw U Tejaniya, Culadasa's The Mind Illuminated and in the Mahasi tradition. She emphasises joy as an integral part of this path to liberation.

Li-Anne's website: www.freeingourmind.com.

BONUS MATERIAL

Get Off Your Cushion Companion Course

To help you further explore the themes of this book, I've created a **FREE** *Companion Course* for you. This includes a downloadable PDF to remind you how easy it is to take your stress and anxiety down a notch *off* the cushion. In addition, there is BONUS video content and a guided meditation for you to explore this practice *on* the cushion.

Visit the following link through this QR code to get free access to your *Get Off Your Cushion* bonus material now.

Manufactured by Amazon.com.au
Sydney, New South Wales, Australia